EUROPE/AMERICA
4

A WIDENING ATLANTIC?
DOMESTIC CHANGE & FOREIGN POLICY

EUROPE/AMERICA
4

A WIDENING ATLANTIC?

DOMESTIC CHANGE & FOREIGN POLICY

Andrew J. Pierre, Editor

Ralf Dahrendorf
Theodore C. Sorensen

COUNCIL ON FOREIGN RELATIONS
58 East 68 Street. New York. N.Y. 10021

COUNCIL ON FOREIGN RELATIONS BOOKS

Copyright © 1986 by the Council on Foreign Relations, Inc.
All rights reserved.
Printed in the United States of America.

Library of Congress Cataloging-in-Publication Data

Dahrendorf, Ralf.
    A widening Atlantic?

    (Europe/America ; 4)
        1. Europe—Foreign relations—United States.
2. United States--Foreign relations—Europe.
3. Europe—Civilization—1945-   . 4. United
States—Civilization—1970-   . I. Pierre,
Andrew J. II. Sorensen, Theodore C. III. Title.
IV. Series.
D1065.U5D26   1986   327.7304   86-2264
ISBN 0-87609-011-0

The Project on European-American Relations

Relations between Western Europe and the United States have become more turbulent in recent years. Divergences in interests and perceptions have grown. Many are questioning the fundamental assumptions of the postwar period. There is a broad consensus that the European-American relationship is in a state of transition.

A new generation is emerging and a number of social and cultural changes are under way that are also contributing to this transition. While our common heritage and values set limits on how far we may drift apart, there is an increasing recognition of the divergences between the United States and Europe on such critical issues as defense and arms control, policy toward the Soviet Union, East-West trade and technology transfer, West-West economic relations, North-South issues, and problems outside the NATO area. The challenge for statesmen will be to manage the differences—and where possible create a new Western consensus—in such a way as to enable the Alliance to adapt to new circumstances while preserving its basic character.

The relatively simple world of the postwar period is gone. Americans today appear to have less understanding of European perspectives and Europeans less appreciation of American views. There is much handwringing about the trans-Atlantic malaise, but less constructive thinking about how to manage and, where possible, reduce our differences.

The project is designed to identify and clarify the differences in interests and perspectives affecting critical issues in the European-American relationship, thereby enhancing understanding across the Atlantic. Approximately three issues per year are selected for examination on a rolling basis over a three-year period. The issues are those that are most likely to create friction in the period ahead.

A short book is published on each issue. European and American authors with points of view that differ from each other but represent important strands of thought in their respective societies contribute analyses of the problem and offer their policy prescriptions. We hope that by disaggregating the issues in this manner, we can make a constructive contribution to the Atlantic debate.

An advisory group of Council members, with the participation of European guests, helps to choose the issues and discusses the ideas in the manuscripts prior to publication. They are, however, in no way responsible for the conclusions, which are solely those of the authors.

We would like to thank the Rockefeller Foundation, the Andrew W. Mellon Foundation and the German Marshall Fund of the United States for their assistance in supporting this project.

Cyrus R. Vance

Advisory Group
Project on European-American Relations

Cyrus R. Vance, *Chairman*
Robert D. Hormats, *Vice-Chairman*
Andrew J. Pierre, *Director of Project*
Kay King, *Assistant Director of Project*

David L. Aaron
George W. Ball
Seweryn Bialer
John Brademas
Hodding Carter, III
Robert F. Ellsworth
Murray H. Finley
Richard N. Gardner
Stanley Hoffmann
Robert E. Hunter
Irving Kristol
Jan M. Lodal
Charles S. Maier
Robert S. McNamara
Harald B. Malmgren
Robert E. Osgood
Maynard Parker

William R. Pearce
Robert V. Roosa
Nathaniel Samuels
J. Robert Schaetzel
John W. Seigle
Marshall D. Shulman
Robert B. Silvers
Anthony M. Solomon
Helmut Sonnenfeldt
Joan E. Spero
Ronald Steel
Fritz Stern
John R. Stevenson
John H. Watts, III

Paul H. Kreisberg, *ex officio*

The editor would like to thank Daniel Bell, Suzanne Berger, Kenneth Clark, William Diebold, William Schneider, William Watts and Daniel Yankelovich for their assistance in planning this volume and/or for their helpful comments on drafts of the manuscripts. He would also like to thank Anne Bertelsen, Moira Coughlin, Meg Hardon, David Kellogg, and Rob Valkenier for their assistance in the production of this book.

The project on European-American Relations is under the auspices of the Council's Studies Program.

Already published:
Nuclear Weapons in Europe, *edited by Andrew J. Pierre, with contributions by William G. Hyland, Lawrence D. Freedman, Paul C. Warnke and Karsten D. Voigt.*

Unemployment and Growth in the Western Economies, *edited by Andrew J. Pierre, with contributions by Marina v.N. Whitman, Raymond Barre, James Tobin and Shirley Williams, and an introduction by Robert D. Hormats.*

Third World Instability: Central America as a European- American Issue, *edited by Andrew J. Pierre, with contributions by Fernando Morán, Irving Kristol, Michael D. Barnes, Alois Mertes and Daniel Oduber.*

Contents

About the Authors

Ralf Dahrendorf is Professor of Social Science at the University of Konstanz in the Federal Republic of Germany. From 1974 to 1984 he was Director of the London School of Economics. Mr. Dahrendorf served on the Commission of the European Communities in Brussels, where from 1973 to 1974 he was responsible for research, science and education and from 1970 to 1973 was in charge of EEC foreign trade and foreign relations. A member of the board of the Federal Republic of Germany's Free Democratic Party from 1968 to 1974, he was a member of the Bundestag and Parliamentary State Secretary in the Federal Foreign Office from 1969 to 1970. Prior to his public service, Mr. Dahrendorf held professorships in sociology at the Universities of Konstanz (1966-69), Tübingen (1960-66), and Hamburg (1958-60). Among his recent publications are *Die Chancen der Krise*, *Life Chances* and *Law and Order*.

Theodore C. Sorensen is a senior partner in the New York City law firm of Paul, Weiss, Rifkind, Wharton and Garrison, where his practice since 1966 has focused on international business transactions. He served as national co-chairman of the Hart for President Campaign in 1983-1984; as chairman of the Governor's Panel on the New York State Export Credit Agency in 1982; and on the National Democratic Platform Committee in 1968 and 1980. He was a member of President Jimmy Carter's Advisory Committee for Trade Negotiations from 1978 to 1980, and from 1967 to 1969 was chairman of the United Nations Association Panel on policy toward Europe. In addition, Mr. Sorensen served as Special Counsel to President John F. Kennedy from 1961 to 1963, prior to which he was assistant to then-Senator Kennedy from 1953 to 1961. His five previous books include *Kennedy* and *A Different Kind of Presidency*.

Andrew J. Pierre is a Senior Fellow at the Council on Foreign Relations and the Director of the Project on European-American

Relations. Formerly on the staff of the Brookings Institution and the Hudson Institute, he has taught at Columbia University. In addition, he served with the Department of State as a Foreign Service Officer in Washington and abroad. Mr. Pierre is the author of *The Global Politics of Arms Sales, Nuclear Politics: The British Experience with an Independent Strategic Force, Nuclear Proliferation: A Strategy for Control*, and other works.

Andrew J. Pierre

Introduction

From the outset of this series of books on European-American relations it has been perfectly evident that it would be essential to give attention to the changing domestic base of foreign policy. If there are growing divergences between Europe and America on some of the key issues in world politics, it is not necessarily or solely because of differences in national interests. A major contributing factor, too often overlooked, has been the changes in how people *think* about such matters as the utility of nuclear weapons, the responsibility of the state for providing economic equity, the future of East-West relations, and the relationship between the rich and poor nations of the world.

Each of the issues addressed in this series will be affected by the attitudes, preferences and values of the citizens of the relevant nation. These attitudes provide the underpinnings for specific national policies. This is inherent in the nature of the democracies that are found on the two sides of the Atlantic. It has been impractical, however, to devote sustained attention to attitudinal changes in each of these relatively short books. It would also be, in some ways, redundant, since our usual format is to select authors with differing points of view, who provide contrasting policy prescriptions (and often values) but who reflect important strands of thought in their respective societies.

Nevertheless, we believe it is important to devote one of the approximate ten books in the series specifically to such questions. This book could well have been the first in the series. Among those who follow Atlantic affairs, it has become commonplace to hear that there are social, cultural, intellectual, demographic and other internal factors that are having a major impact upon nations' external relations. There has, in addition, been much talk about the coming into power of a "successor generation" comprised of those individuals who are replacing the

1

founding fathers of the North Atlantic Treaty Organization and the European Communities (EC). The political consequences of the changing domestic factors and of the successor generation are widely, and probably correctly, thought to be of considerable significance. It is striking, therefore, how little analytical inquiry and sustained scholarly attention has been given to these phenomena, despite the conventional wisdom about their importance.

This volume presents the personal reflections of two seasoned, and I believe wise, observers of their respective societies. Rather than having four or five authors, as in the other books in the series, we thought that the subject could better be addressed through two longer, and wider ranging, essays. Both Ralf Dahrendorf and Theodore C. Sorensen are individuals who combine serious intellectual inquiry with practical political experience. Both know their respective societies extremely well: Dahrendorf as a West German who recently completed ten years as the Director of the London School of Economics, after having been an EC commissioner in Brussels; and Sorensen as Special Counsel to President John F. Kennedy, a long time observer of the American political scene and national co-chairman of Senator Gary Hart's 1984 presidential campaign, which sought to develop the "new ideas" attractive to a younger generation of voters.

In recent times there has been some discussion of a "widening Atlantic." This concept is meant to indicate that perceptions and interests, as viewed on either side of the ocean, are pulling Europe and America apart. How valid is this concept?

In asking this question we immediately confront a paradox. On the one hand, the intensity of communications across the Atlantic has never been greater as measured by jet travel, direct-dial telephone, the telex, satellite television that permits conversations linking individuals and audiences on the two continents, and simultaneous publication of the same daily newspapers.

On the other hand, there appears to be less understanding about each other's societies, political systems and foreign policy interests than even a decade or two ago. As our societies have become more complex, the "knowledge gap" has increased despite the advances in communication and the growth of tourism.

As a result it often appears as if irritability has risen and tolerance decreased. People are quicker to accept distorted and even wrong images as reality: the trigger-happy cowboy of American diplomacy or the spineless, narrow-minded European.

The notion of a widening Atlantic has some basis in fact:

• since 1983 American trade with Western Europe has been less than with the countries of the Pacific Basin;

• the percentage of the American population living in the western states has doubled since World War II, thereby creating a shift in the political center of gravity toward the Sunbelt and away from the eastern and northern states that traditionally were considered to have been more Europe-oriented;

• the proportion of Americans who do not look back on a European origin (blacks, hispanics and Asians) has changed from one in ten in the 1940s to almost one in four today;

• Europeans no longer view the United States as a model society, one that they wish to emulate, as they did in the first postwar decades;

• the emerging generation of European political leaders is less likely than previous ones to include individuals who have spent a year or two in an American university;

• Europeans are increasingly conscious of their common concerns, from the environment to high technology to arms control, and this has led to a marked expansion of intra-European contacts in the private sector and a deepening of consultations among governments.

Yet at another, and less quantifiable, level the ties that bind remain strong. A common heritage, a shared system of values, and a joint commitment to democracy—in addition to a continuing concern about security and a deep economic interdependency—set limits on the extent to which the two sides of the Atlantic can drift apart.

Whether or not the Atlantic is widening, the character of relations between Europe and the United States may increasingly be dependent upon domestic changes within our respective societies. Our hope is that these two essays on the "Europeanization of Europe" and "A Changing America" will assist the reader in forming his or her own judgment concerning the future.

December 1985

Ralf Dahrendorf

The Europeanization of Europe

The trouble with change in human affairs is that it is so hard to pin down. It happens all the time. But while it happens it eludes our grasp, and once we feel able to come to grips with it, it has become past history. (After all, the owl of Minerva begins its flight at dusk.) In the meantime, almost anything goes. Some argue that there have always been strains in European-American relations, and there are today, but in fact the Alliance remains as strong as ever. Others say that the gap between Europe and America has widened to the point at which the cohesion of the Alliance is at risk. They cannot both be right, though they might both be wrong. In any case, they remind us of the need for caution.

The Alliance is real, and it is necessary in my view. What changes there are, do not affect its core. Yet there are changes. Since the early 1970s, there has been a significant Americanization of America, and simultaneously, if more haltingly, a certain Europeanization of Europe. The process is bound to have an effect, though what exactly it is, or should be, is as yet unclear.

The subject of this analysis is Europe. Moreover, it is the domestic background of Europe's international stance, notably in relation to the United States. Thus, this is an essay about social, economic and political change. The story begins with the economic miracle of the postwar years, the convulsions of 1968 and 1973, and the dilemma of economic security and flexibility. It continues to the political sphere and the rise and fall of social democracy. But one must make a distinction between which Europe is being examined, as there are important differences within the critical boundaries. The fact that the European Community (EC) comprises only a part of Europe does not necessar-

5

ily make it less important, but even so, European integration raises many questions that are addressed. The Atlantic Alliance itself is the subject of the concluding discussion. Throughout the essay, the links between domestic change and foreign policy are shown.

The Americanization of America

My thesis is that Europe is becoming more European. But there is an analogous process taking place on the other side of the Atlantic, the Americanization of America, and the two are undoubtedly related. It may provide a useful backcloth, therefore, if America is examined first. America in this connection is of course—and with an apology to those many other Americans— the United States. The first markers of a process that is still very much with us were set, not by Ronald Reagan, nor by Mike Mansfield, but by former Secretary of the Treasury John Connally and the seemingly internationalist Richard Nixon. August 15, 1971, remains a date to remember, especially at a time in which "disequilibria" of the balances of trade and of payments are once again in the forefront of domestic and international debate.

The story of August 15, 1971, is familiar. After months in which then-Under Secretary of the Treasury Paul Volcker had America's partners to take voluntary action in order to assist the United States to balance its deficits, the President and his Treasury Secretary announced what in Japan came to be called, the "Nixon shocks": the suspension of the convertibility of the dollar into gold as well as certain specific measures designed to boost American exports (by tax concessions) and to limit foreign imports (by a surtax). Not all measures announced on August 15, 1971, were destined for a long life. The General Agreement on Tariffs and Trade (GATT), where the memory of the Kennedy Round was still fresh, managed to assert its principles (and thus, incidentally, pave the way for a new trade negotiation, which was first called, the Nixon Round, only to be renamed the Tokyo Round after Watergate). The U.S. government revoked most trade restrictions in the autumn of 1971. On the other hand, the Smithsonian Agreement of December 1971 led to a realignment of major currencies but failed to live up to the President's epithet "historic" in that it did not establish a new monetary system to take the place of that of Bretton Woods.

However, it is not just specific measures of monetary and commercial policy that make the Nixon shocks of 1971 memorable, rather it is their underlying philosophy. In a near paraphrase of Secretary Connally's words, this philosophy was that the United States no longer saw any reason to bear a disproportionate share of the burden of an international system that it, above all others, had created and upheld. Since then the United States has found it easier than before to define its interests in a narrow national sense rather than in terms of wider international responsibilities. It is true that the outcome of the Law of the Sea Conference called for difficult compromises such as the substitution of an "authority" for the "market," but the United States had been actively engaged in the negotiations from the outset. Without doubt, a "new world information order" has little to do with the original, liberal objectives of the U.N. Educational, Scientific and Cultural Organization, and even if the project is dropped, it tells a story; but the withdrawal of the most important founder member hardly helps the rest. Of course, judgments of the International Court of Justice may be awkward; but rejecting its jurisdiction is more serious still. For what kind of world order are we going to live by if the most powerful nation of the world reacts to the discovery that international arrangements are inconvenient largely by invoking a particular, often narrow, view of immediate interests?

This is a comment where analysis is needed first. Turning from Secretary Connally to Senator Mansfield, we encounter the familiar American theme of isolationism. It is probably the oldest theme of American foreign policy: "as little political connection as possible with foreign nations," was a maxim of George Washington's. But there are differences. There is the confident isolationism of a country concentrating on building a world that is free of the misery and persecution of the countries from which its citizens had come. There is the disdainful isolationism of a country that believes others are hankering after values, geopolitical values for example, that are alien to its own tradition and creed. And there is the fearful, anxious isolationism of a country that does not mind beggaring its neighbors or letting them down for that matter, in order to preserve its own precarious position. Such anxious isolationism is at issue today.

Beggar-thy-neighbor is a term of art, or rather of the artlessness of the 1930s. It was then applied to trade. Trade probably does not tie nations together as firmly as its advocates pretend to believe. Many a trade link has been severed within days when it suited one side or the other. Trade is in many respects a fair-weather phenomenon. But it is at least indicative not just of the climate, but of what people make of it. If they begin to talk of "fair" rather than free trade, of "responsible" rather than liberal policies, of "orderly marketing" rather than markets, then something has snapped. Uncertain growth expectation, depressed industries and regions, unemployment or the threat of it, are strong motives for "me first" attitudes, whether they advocate "Britain first," "Australia first," or "America first." It helps little to repeat that such attitudes are usually self-defeating. The battle between the short and the medium term is almost always won by the former. Adam Smith knew this, and it has been the sadness of liberals ever since. The important point is that once an inward-looking posture born out of fear prevails, it becomes that much more difficult to maintain a climate of open and confident cooperation.

It would be more than a little misleading to describe the Americanization of America as a largely negative process. To be sure, the country's tendency to turn to its immediate interests has had some unfortunate international ramifications, and we have probably not seen the end of them. Current American attitudes toward Japanese imports are ominous, as are recurrent congressional threats to the World Bank, and a recent inclination to present allies with faits accomplis rather than proposals. But there is a brighter side to the picture of an America concentrating on itself rather than the world around. It is President Reagan's side, as it were, that continues to impress not only America's voters but also its friends.

In the mid 1980s, the domestic problems of the countries of the free world are similar, however different their specific incarnations may be. One problem is, the relation between what have come to be called the public and the private "sectors" of society. Its most important aspect has to do with the social state—the "welfare state"—and the relative role of public expenditure and private savings, though this is only a part of the issue that stands for the whole. A second problem arises from the nature and the future of work in societies that assume for all practical purposes that paid employment is the basis of people's social existence but that have gone out of their way to reduce the burden of work in the name of freedom. As a result, there is much to do, but not enough paid employment to go around. The new unemployment may be no more than a symptom, but it is a symptom of a profound change that affects more than our language. Are we on the road to a post-capitalist, post-industrial, post-modern society? The third, and arguably the most difficult, problem touches on the social contract itself. It is no accident that "law and order" has become an issue. From the incidence of muggings and burglaries to riots and violent demonstrations, from the emergence of vigilante groups to the spread of the "black economy" there are numerous expressions of doubt about the validity—the legitimacy?—of the social and political order by which we are trying to live.

Several answers to the problems of the day are on offer. There are those pragmatists who believe that the problems are but temporary aberrations, conjunctural perhaps, and that basically we are on the right path. There are others who want us to be more forthright in pursuing the course of recent decades, the traditional reformers. Both pragmatists and traditional reformers represent versions of what might be called, social democracy, though neither of them is very convincing. But then, what is?

This is where the recent history of the United States provides at least food for thought. For in America almost everyone seems agreed that if only the old American values could be revived, all would be well. These are a combination of self-reliance and the morality of non-indulgence, thus of hard work and the willingness to wait for the pleasures of achievement, of flexibility and puritanism. What matters is not to reform society but to prove one's mettle in the competitive struggle of life. The fittest will survive, and will even spare a thought for the "deserving poor." Basically, people work on the assumption that they are the masters of their own destiny, and that there are no free lunches to be had. Richard Hofstadter has described these values in his early work *Social Darwinism in American Thought*, and has also added the telling point, "We may wonder whether, in the entire history of thought, there was ever a conservatism so utterly progressive as this."[1]

There are variants of the American creed. But President Reagan's appeal to the country's traditional values has been singularly successful. This is remarkable. In Europe, there is no equivalent to this process. When British Prime Minister Margaret Thatcher tried a similar line of attack, she was almost bound to fail. What values was she to resurrect? Despite some myths to the contrary, Victorian England was not another America. As Martin Wiener has recently reminded us, and Alfred Marshall had noted long before, the industrial spirit in England declined almost as soon as it rose.[2] If anything, the English tradition is one of pre-industrial aristocratic values. Elsewhere in Europe, the coziness—the rigidity—of the premodern world may have blended differently with the competitiveness of the industrial age, but the mixture is still characteristic, and it shows that in this respect at least, America is unique. It is the country where the often painful, but always remarkable effort that has brought people across hostile seas to its shores has remained a motive force for later generations.

Thus, the Americanization of America is in one sense a return to the founts of tradition. America's new patriotism is quite genuine, and it makes sense to say that the country is getting going *again*. Except, of course, that as we step into the same waters we soon discover that they are not really the same. One can remind oneself of history, even revive some of its motives, but one cannot repeat it. The last frontiers closed some time ago, and no Silicon Valley will re-open them. Even the self-reliant American of the 1980s cannot escape the strangling Laokoon-like struggle with rules and regulations, lawyers and government officials. Many a heavy hand in both the public and private sectors

---

[1] Richard Hofstadter, *Social Darwinism in American Thought*, Boston: Beacon Press, 1955, p. 8.

[2] Martin Wiener, *English Culture and the Decline of the Industrial Spirit 1850–1980*, Cambridge: Cambridge University Press, 1981.

holds the enterprising individual back. The return to tradition cannot suspend history.

This point applies more generally: the United States may be a superpower *malgré lui*, but it is inevitably involved in the four corners of the world. American military power and political will determine whether there is peace or war. The dollar continues to be a ubiquitous yardstick of economic strength, Bretton Woods or not. When progress of any kind, not just technological advance, is the issue, people look to the United States, whatever they may say about the newly and not so newly industrializing countries of Asia. Without American help, national, transnational and international, the Third World would be in an even more hopeless state. Moreover, there are international organizations, there is an Atlantic Alliance; and these are sustained in every sense of the word by the United States. All this may not engender love for American power; but then international affairs are not about love, but about interest. Whether they like it or not, America needs the world, and the world needs America.

This means that the Americanization of America since the early 1970s has not altered the basic substance of the international system; but it has changed its flavor. Perhaps it can be said that the singular position of the United States in world affairs has become even more apparent. There is rather less emphasis today on common institutional constraints and more on particular, by their very nature unilateral, interests. The Pax Americana of the postwar world, a more or less organized international system, which was both accepted and guaranteed by the United States, has retreated somewhat in favor of a more outright exercise of power by those who have it. This was never absent of course. Still, nuances do make a difference. At the very least, the Americanization of America forces, or perhaps encourages, others to seek their own ways. Perhaps, this is the heart of the story that this essay is trying to tell—the story of Europe.

Economy and Society: A European Syndrome

For most Europeans, the economic explosion of the postwar decades came as a surprise. The ups and downs of the interwar years were still fresh on people's minds. The prevailing view was that the golden age had ended in 1913 and that the most one could hope for was a plodding, difficult process of reconstruction. The Marshall Plan extended an imaginative and generous helping hand across the Atlantic; but neither those who held it out nor those who were delighted to grasp it could expect it to release the economic energies that were in fact set free. For between the immediate postwar years and the early 1970s, a quality change took place in people's standard of living and in the capacity of economies to sustain it. In that quarter-century, memories of an earlier golden age were wiped out and replaced by a new experience.

If this sounds lyrical, it is not inappropriate. The 1950s and 1960s were, in Walt Rostow's words, "the most remarkable two decades of economic growth in modern history."[3] He might as well have said, in history. Never before have so many seen their economic life chances improve so much in such a short time. There were differences—there always are when one speaks about Europe—but by the early 1970s very few people anywhere in Europe were not significantly better off than they, or their families, had been in the late 1940s.

Among the side effects of the economic miracle, not the least important was that it brought Europe and the United States closer together. This was true in a technical sense. Whereas in the major countries of Europe, real gross national product grew (between 1955 and 1972) an average of six percent each year, American growth rates over the same period were closer to four percent; in other words, Europe began to catch up. But beyond technicalities, Europeans learned to play positive-sum games, an old American pastime. Whatever problems arose, there were always solutions that made everyone happier, albeit with gradations of bliss. One was always looking forward to new frontiers rather than fighting about the old ones. Apart from growth itself, a growth mentality spread. This engendered certain international interests, which Americans and Europeans shared. The Kennedy Round of trade liberalization measures marks the high

---

[3]Walt W. Rostow, *The World Economy: History and Prospect,* London: Macmillan, 1978, p. 247.

point of this community of interest. Needless to say, there were problems too, economic and, above all, political; but by and large there were also solutions, and these were often agreed upon or at least in keeping with each other.

In the early 1970s, the scene changed drastically. The Nixon shocks of 1971 were but one of the milestones on this road. In 1972, the Club of Rome published its first report on the *Limits to Growth.* Nineteen seventy-three was the year of the Yom Kippur War and the first oil shock. Almost everywhere, inflation had begun to reveal a growing gap between aspirations and realities. Coupled with stagnation, it produced the new threat of stagflation. And the paths of Europe and America began to part.

This new departure is not primarily the result of the change of scene in the early 1970s, but is the product of another transformation. We shall call it, "1968." For most of Europe, 1968 is a date of some significance. While a revolution was not as imminent elsewhere as it may have been for a few tense days in May of that year in Paris, a sea change of prevailing moods, and more, took place all over Europe. In this transformation, Vietnam played its part, though more as a symbol than as a cause. It was an indigenous European process. Since it cannot really be linked to one particular year, it might be better to speak of "1968" rather than 1968.

As the 1960s progressed, there emerged, in many parts of Europe, a sense that economic growth was not enough. After a period of expansion, reforms were needed; after a time of quantitative economic advances one looked for qualitative social changes. People began to seek a better life and not just more of the same thing. This sounds vague, and much of the debate at the time was somewhat nebulous. Yet it had certain themes and lasting aftereffects.

The themes have tinny names, which have since entered everyday language: redistribution, democratization, participation. The welfare state of postwar Europe was, in a sense, both a response to the trauma of the 1930s and an expression of the social consensus of the war years. In the 1960s however, it received a new impetus. Some of its gaps, apparent or real, were filled. A dimension of civic equality, of extended citizenship rights, was added in the name of democracy. While protagonists claimed they were after equality of opportunity, the boundary at which this turns into equality of results became blurred—and not only in education. Emphasis on participation was both specific, as in the case of industrial "co-determination," and general, as in the emergence of "citizens' initiatives" and situational politics.

These themes are familiar to North Americans. From John Kenneth Galbraith's demand to create a better balance between "private wealth" and "public squalor" to John Rawls's plea for "justice as fairness," there is an influential literature and the "Great Society" has provided at least some scope for application.[4] Yet "1968" left a more lasting and a deeper imprint in Europe. To be sure, it did not happen everywhere at the same time and in the same way. In France, the moment of bated breath passed, and when a socialist president came to power in 1981, the rose of hope looked strangely out of place in an environment of constraints. In Great Britain, the vagaries of the electoral system led first to the episode of Prime Minister Edward Heath and his U-turn from neo-Darwinism to traditional conservatism, and then to the unhappy governments of Harold Wilson in 1974, torn between half-hearted socialism and the demands of the International Monetary Fund. Only West German Chancellor Willy Brandt's coalition government of 1969 set out explicitly to "venture more democracy," though it too reached the end of this particular tether when Helmut Schmidt became chancellor in 1974. There were other stories. The countries of the Iberian Peninsula and the eastern Mediterranean were still in the throes of authoritarian rule. Scandinavia had already seen decades of social democracy. But if one looks back on this period and through the formal changes of government, one feature stands out. The phase of reform resulted in a significant strengthening of the public sphere of economic and social life. What had begun with John Maynard Keynes and William Beveridge, with the application of the *General Theory of Employment, Interest and Money*, and with *Full Employment in a Free Society*, ended with a new role of the state and its servants. After "1968," one must

---

[4]John Kenneth Galbraith, *The Affluent Society*, Cambridge, Mass.: Riverside Press, 1958; and John Rawls, *The Theory of Justice*, London: Oxford University Press, 1972.

wonder whether it makes much sense to describe the economies and societies of Europe as capitalist.

The process has many facets: a considerable extension of government's tool box of economic policy, rising levels of direct and indirect taxation, legislation to restrict the use of private property and protect employees and tenants, and ever more numerous entitlements from the public purse are some of them. But easily the most significant aspect from a political standpoint, has to do with the rapid growth of the public service class and its mentality. In West Germany, the number of public servants has doubled between 1970 and 1985; two-and-a-half million people now have all the perks and rights of civil servants. Millions of others occupy analogous positions. Their incomes are indexed in practice, if not in theory; they cannot be dismissed, and if anyone tries there will be a "labor court" to reverse the decision; they are looked after, if not from the cradle, then from the date of first employment, to the grave. Looked after by whom? They look after themselves, of course. The case of Sweden may be exceptional even in Europe. There, 28 percent of the population are public servants, and another 24 percent live primarily on their social entitlements. A majority of the electorate depends on public money. The principle is the same all over Europe. The number of people whose life chances depend directly on government, central or local, or on para-governmental agencies, has grown by leaps and bounds. What is more, it is this category that sets the tone. European societies have become public-service societies.

In other words, 1968 did not last, but "1968" did. The age of reform quickly came to an end, but its effect is still very much with us, even when the 1970s ended a quarter-century of positive-sum games. Indeed, since social trends are no more easily stopped or deflected than modern supertankers—*The Inertia of the Tanker* is the title of a political analysis by the secretary general of the West German Social Democrats.[5] The extension of the public service and its attendant mentality continued long into the period in which the agenda of politics had changed. Helmut Schmidt knew this and so did Great Britain's Prime Minister

---

[5]Peter Glotz, *Die Unbeweglichkeit des Tankers*, Munich: Bertelsmann, 1982.

James Callaghan and France's President Valéry Giscard d'Estaing. They were all reformers at heart, but they recognized that the new task was to stop the rot and then look for futures. First, inflation had to be curbed, and public expenditure brought under control, then new sources of innovation had to be opened up, and finally, the necessary adjustments had to be effected. This was not popular. So they achieved little, and in the end all three lost their majorities. One might even say that "Eurosclerosis" defeated them. There were other reasons. In any case, their successors faced the same problems.

Mancur Olson combined a Scandinavian background with American experience (and a great deal of thought and analysis) when he wrote his *Rise and Decline of Nations.* The book is an indictment of the social and economic rigidities that have befallen so many "old" countries. Olson makes careful distinctions. He documents the differences between the Federal Republic of Germany and Great Britain, or between East and West, North and South in the United States. Yet his book reads like a preliminary case history of what has come to be called the "European disease." Societies whose economies become too rigid to adjust, innovate and grow, are doomed. They will fall into a long winter of medieval rigor, from which only drastic and painful changes can awaken them. ("We can also appreciate anew Thomas Jefferson's observation that 'the tree of liberty must be refreshed from time to time with the blood of patriots and tyrants.' ")[6] The danger of stagflation, and ungovernability in its wake, is great wherever coalitions of special-interest groups have managed to get rules and practices adopted that make their economies inflexible and ill-adapted to the needs of forever changing markets. Olson adds insult to injury when he explains the "logic of his argument," which is "that countries that have had democratic freedom of organization without upheaval or invasion the longest will suffer the most from growth-repressing organizations and combinations."[7] This is clearly aimed at Great Britain.

---

[6]Mancur Olson, *The Rise and Decline of Nations: Economic Growth, Stagflation and Social Rigidities*, New Haven: Yale University Press, 1982, p. 141.

[7]*Ibid.*, p. 77.

But what about Switzerland? Or Sweden? Olson's case is strong. Much of it could be applied to the syndrome that we have called, "1968." But there remains a niggling doubt, even with respect to Great Britain. Could it not be that the case against Eurosclerosis that has become so fashionable could be turned into one for Eurostrength?

Europe has had a difficult decade. Since the mid-1970s, uncertain prospects of economic growth have come to be combined with reductions in the benefits of the social state and new problems for which solutions are hard to find. These new problems include stagflation and more recently, boom unemployment— that is, unemployment that refuses to go away as economies begin to look up. Governments everywhere had to ask for a new austerity; political parties no longer raised but dampened expectations. In trying to explain the predicament, those whose interests are obvious were by no means the only ones to use Olson's language. Europe has aged; a kind of socio-economic arteriosclerosis has set in; flexibility is absent and innovation hard to come by. The old continent is falling behind the United States and, above all, Japan. Unless the remedies of supply-side economics, the encouragement of innovation and investment by lower taxes are adopted soon, Europe is going to fall irretrievably behind. But is it?

It is certainly true that the economies of most European countries have been more sluggish in finding a way out of the depressing early 1980s than either the United States or Japan. It is also true that there has been less of an upbeat mood in Europe: "Eurogloom" has not exactly encouraged investment, or the process of adjustment in general. It could be argued moreover that in Europe there has been as much debate about innovation as actual innovation, and the debate has often been laden with doubts and qualms. Clearly, what we have called the public-service mentality has not helped; flexibility has not been the order of the day.

But there is another side to the picture. Arguably, the European recovery in recent years is not as precarious as that of the United States. It is not based on borrowed money (though the exchange rate of the dollar has helped), nor is it as close to the margin of high risk, nor is it accompanied by a sense that it cannot last much longer either. There has been, in many parts of Europe, an attempt to find new syntheses—economy and ecology, work and environment, participation and flexibility—that are alien to the textbooks of neo-liberal economics, but that may not be all bad. And so far as innovation is concerned, a surprising amount has happened, both at the frontiers of research and development, and in the transformation of industrial processes. The fact that the process of deindustrialization tends to be slower in Europe than in the United States, may yet turn out to be a source of strength.

This could even be the case with respect to the public-service mentality. In terms of a narrow economic concept of welfare, this mentality and the institutions that go with it, must clearly appear as obstacles. People who are rendered immobile by a battery of social policies ranging from employment protection to housing subsidies, are hardly the stuff from which an innovative, rapidly adjusting economy is made. But they may be happy, even without dramatic rates of growth in real incomes or gross domestic product. Some would argue that this is precisely what decadence is about. However, happy people may in the end be a better guarantee of sustained economic and social progress than unhappy people who are continuing in the rat race. At least in Europe this may be the case.

It is a striking fact that the most successful European countries in recent years have also been the ones furthest away from the American model. Neither Austria nor Sweden nor Switzerland will delight supply-side economists. The first two have had social-democratic governments, the third, insofar as it had a government at all, a coalition including the (moderate) right as well as the (moderate) left. In all three, a considerable degree of social cohesion extends into relations between business and labor as well as between government, the banks and the partners of industry. Elements of such relations can be found all over Europe.

No one has ever doubted that the success of Japan is not based on the application of the American model. Talking of Japan and the United States in the same breath, as if they were examples of flexibility and innovative spirit, is more than a little misleading. In parts of the United States, there may still be a true sense of openness and self-reliance: flexible flexibility as it were. But the

Japanese experience has plausibly been described as one of "flexible rigidity"; Japan operates "beyond market capitalism."[8] The net effect may be one of flexibility, but this is brought about by people in highly rigid positions reacting to signals that no outsider could understand. If the Japanese move toward new horizons, the cause is more likely to be found in the Ministry of International Trade and Industry (MITI) and the Employers' Association (*Keidanren*) than in incentives or the search for open frontiers. The information technology adjustment provides a supreme example.

It may be that there is a third—i.e., European—pattern of success. This would not involve collectivities in the way that Japanese society does, nor would it leave individuals to fend for themselves in the American manner. It would be a combination of individual security guaranteed by the solidarity of the community, and individual effort stimulated by incentives and other market forces. To call it rigid flexibility is perhaps too much of a play on words; it is in any case more a combination of basic security with flexibility, economic flexibility with reduced social stakes.

There are, we have argued, three major social problems today. One is, the future of the social state. Significant changes in its organization, its level and method of finance, and even in the relative weight of public and private contributions are bound to take place all over Europe. But it is likely that these changes will involve the reassertion rather than the abandonment of Beveridge's fundamental principle that all citizens should be entitled to a decent standard of living. The second problem is work. It is most unlikely that any European government will be able to rely for long on the operation of (labor) market forces to restore full employment. The more probable development is one that will, in important respects, lead beyond the confines of the work society. Work-sharing, flexible retirement, community service, alternative economic ventures, a flourishing "black economy" and many other methods will serve to combine employment

---

[8]Thus says Ronald Dore of the London Technical Change Centre; see *Beyond Market Capitalism,* a lecture by Dore published under the auspices of the London School of Economics in 1983.

with activity. And when it comes to the third problem, law and order, or the new social contract, it is quite clear that in Europe it will have more clauses than American constitutional economists approve of.

The gist of these remarks is that Europe has its own peculiar strengths. These become evident at a time of crisis. While it is fashionable to compare oneself with the United States, and even Japan, success is more likely to lie on a road that does not start in nowhere, but in the history of the old continent. At the moment, comparisons abound. They lead to the diagnosis of Eurosclerosis, and the reaction of Eurogloom. But there are signs of a new European confidence, and what is more, there are reasons for it. Europe can turn its apparent weaknesses into strengths and hold its own in the world.

If this happens—and to some extent it has happened already—it will have a profound effect on relations between Europe and America. The postwar boom was not only a common experience, but also one that led to joint action. "1968" was a very European story, even if it had American ingredients and in its turn reverberated all over the world. The socio-economic challenges of the 1980s will bring out similar, but also divergent forces. Prime Minister Thatcher was not the only one to prescribe American medicines for Europe; in West Germany, the then-Economics Minister Otto Lambsdorff and the Minister President of Lower Saxony Ernst Albrecht tried the same in the early 1980s. They tried in vain. The balance between public and private, between solidarity and individual effort, is different in Europe. The result is a curious ambiguity of prevailing sentiments. A leading European politician was heard to say privately, "Wouldn't it be nice to spend half the year in America, and half in Europe?" Wouldn't it be nice, in other words, to enjoy the sense of adventure and movement and freedom of Texas and California some of the time but that of belonging and history and security for the remainder? In reality, the differences are not as stark. There are very European parts of the United States, and almost American parts of Europe. But the turning point of "1968" is not something that can be undone in Europe; it was too much in line with long-standing traditions. The question is therefore how a balance can be struck between mutuality and difference in Atlantic trends.

Political Trends

The single-most significant European political development since the end of World War II has been the emergence of a broad consensus around views that can best be described as social democratic. Naturally, the rise of the social democratic consensus was a slow and incomplete process. Also, its pace and character differed from one country to another. Moreover, it did not last. But for decades, it set the tone of politics. To some extent it still does; though today, the more interesting question is whether (and if so where) there are new forces that may foreshadow a different future.

In one sense, democratic politics is always about the center. Whoever gains it or keeps it, despite reaching out for new horizons, can be sure of finding a majority. But over time, the center itself is shifting. In the postwar world, it has shifted slowly, but perceptibly to the left. Domestically the new consensus was characterized by the names of Keynes and Beveridge. The former stood for a benevolent state mitigating the effects of conjunctural changes in economic fortune, the latter for a beneficent state mitigating the distributive effects of unfettered market processes. The state as policymaker and the state as redistributor have come to the fore everywhere. In terms of political style, the explicit search for consensus between opposing interests was part-and-parcel of the social democratic approach. Internationally the experience of totalitarianism, and therefore the desire to defend the open society, has been the dominant motive. Support for the postwar international system, but also for the Western Alliance within it, has resulted from this motive.

The dominance of a social democratic center of this persuasion was not easily achieved. Memories of the terrible division of the interwar period lingered on. It took some time for the "democratic class struggle" (as Seymour Martin Lipset has called it[9]) to develop—that is to say for historical all-or-nothing battles to turn into civilized campaign fights and parliamentary debates. Still, by the mid-1950s, authors in many countries thought that the

---

[9]Seymour Martin Lipset, *Political Man: The Social Bases of Politics,* Garden City, N.Y.: Doubleday, 1960, chap. vii.

"end of ideology" had arrived, and that we were in for a long period of reasonable, even rational politics (very social democratic concepts these!). The time of strife, so it seemed, was over.

Developments in different countries were characteristically different in detail but also remarkably parallel in structure. In Great Britain, the apparently radical departures of the 1945 Labour government were in fact tolerated by the Conservatives. Even in 1951, Churchill stated that "socialist legislation" had to be allowed to "reach its full fruition."[10] There followed the period of "Butskellism," named after the respective Conservative and Labour Prime Ministers Rab Butler and Hugh Gaitskell, whose policies were virtually indistinguishable. Harold Macmillan had always sought the "middle way." In any case, a kind of corporatism grew in Great Britain, which was to find its climax and turning point in Harold Wilson's "social contract" between government and the unions.

In West Germany, the early years of the second democratic venture were years of vicious political conflict. Two views of reconstruction, and of the Federal Republic's international role, clashed in the persons of Konrad Adenauer and the leader of the Social Democratic Party (SPD), Kurt Schumacher. But in the 1950s, the conflict subsided. The Social Democrats made their peace with gradualism at home (in the Godesberg Program of 1959) and with the Western Alliance abroad (in Herbert Wehner's Bundestag speech of 1960). There followed a period that culminated in a "grand coalition" of Social and Christian Democrats; attempts at "concerted action" between business, labor and government; and, interrupted only by the beginning of *Ostpolitik,* a general move toward consensus around the new center.

The French story is less simple. Was the Fourth Republic a case of consensus politics or of adversary politics? Still, Charles de Gaulle managed to rally the nation a second time, and characteristically, both Presidents Valéry Giscard d'Estaing and François Mitterrand have tried to reach across the right-left divide

---

[10]Speech after the 1951 Conservative Party election victory, quoted in Arthur Seldon, *Churchill's Indian Summer,* London: Hodder & Stoughton, 1976, p. 437.

and appeal to the great majority of Frenchmen. They may have failed on the level of pure politics, but their intention seemed to meet a perceived need. This is true in Italy, too, where the notion of a "historic compromise" between the two largest parties, the Christian Democrats and the Communists, has left important traces on both. Europe's smaller countries are in any case more consensus-prone. Austria's "black-red coalitions"; the "magic formula" by which Switzerland's Federal Council is constituted (two Liberals, two Social Democrats, two Christians, one People's Party representative); and the, for the outsider at least, near-indistinguishability of the policies of governments and oppositions in Scandinavia are but examples.

This is not the whole story of postwar politics in Europe. Regional and sectarian conflicts continued to tear some countries apart. In others, the major part of the postwar era was taken up by the fight for democracy itself. But by and large, the free governments of Europe were shaped politically by the search for a social democratic consensus. Its progress was the political equivalent of the socio-economic processes of reconstruction and of reform. In the end, a majority class had emerged whose members could envisage the realization of most of their aspirations even if nothing changed very much. Then, the storms of the 1970s broke loose. This is not the place to examine in detail whether their origins were primarily exogenous (like the oil shocks, or even the Nixon shocks), or homemade. Inflation was not the only phenomenon in which both sets of factors converged. What became increasingly clear was that the social democratic consensus was not sufficient to cope with a new socio-economic environment.

A period of tinkering began, of small and, wherever possible, painless adjustments to a changed climate. Here, pensioners were asked to make a small contribution to health care; there, student grants were in part transformed into loans; everywhere, some support for the construction industry was coupled with some tax relief for all. To some extent, this period of tinkering still continues. But the notion has gained ground that such minor repairs of the system are not enough. The style of politics has become harsher. The end of social democracy is in sight, and new political forces have emerged.

These are not so much the forces of the traditional right or left. It is striking and worth noting that even today, the interwar period looks like an episode, albeit one of the most costly episodes in human history. Its political faultings have not recurred. To be sure, every now and again, when the center evacuates the right wing too obviously, or when a new "leader" appears to emerge, parties of the traditional right make some headway. West German National Democrats got close to five percent of the popular vote in 1969; in the mid-1980s, National Front Leader Jean-Marie Le Pen is reviving a time-honored French tradition; football hooliganism and racial violence are linked to the National Front in Great Britain. But there is no indication whatever of a new Nazi party making significant gains anywhere in Europe.

The traditional left in turn is reduced to the status of a vociferous sect. Unlike the right, it is much in evidence through its publications; though one is struck by the fact that perhaps for the first time since the French Revolution it is no longer true to say in Europe that *der Geist weht links*. Wherever the spirit bends, it is not in the academic or organizational circles of a left that is characterized by a pathetic insistence that nothing has changed and capitalism is still the main enemy. Not only are authors of the left losing their readers, but two other developments have taken place all over Europe. One is that authors of quality have turned away from the left. Once again, their god has failed, though this time it was a minor god that has failed because it has become boring. Its name must be some combination of Beveridge and Keynes. In France, in Italy, in Great Britain, in West Germany, there is a whole new literature by disenchanted social democrats. The other related development is that parties of the formerly extreme left have first turned social democratic themselves and then lost their fascination for those who used to support them. The cases of the Italian and French Communist Parties warrant a separate analysis in this connection. In both countries, such an analysis would probably show that the new linkages of the class struggles of industrial Europe, those of a consciously organized proletariat, lost their strength in the 1960s and 1970s. The same is true in Great Britain, which outsiders still like to describe in traditional class terms, but which in fact has seen the gradual weakening of class ties as social democracy advanced. Intellectually as well as politically, the title of a book by the German Marxist, Jurgen Habermas, *Die neue Unubersichtlichkeit*, describes as well as anything what has happened to the left: the new obscurity, the new impossibility (or incapacity?) to make sense of things are all possible renderings of the title.

It would be wrong not to mention in this connection the fact that Europe has been subject to waves of terrorism. By this is not meant the Irish problem with its long and involuted history, nor even the Basque problem for which there are precedents, but the emergence of anarchist groups on the left and organized gangs on the right, such as the Red Army Faction in West Germany or Direct Action in France, and also the skinheads in Great Britain and similar groups elsewhere. It is both tempting and misleading to explain organized crime in general terms simply because it has political aspirations and overtones. Still, it could be argued that whenever attempts to open up the entrenched political system are seen to fail by those who make them, a small group goes down the well-trodden path of symbolic violence. Institutions and their representatives are attacked in order to demonstrate problems rather than to change things in constitutional ways. This was true after 1968; it may again be true if the West German Green Party, and comparable groupings elsewhere, decline further; it is inherently true for the isolated political sects of the right.

And let there be no mistake: violence is one response to the underlying problems of the 1970s and 1980s. As social democratic tinkering is seen to be more and more inadequate, some people get very angry with the world of predictability and security. One remembers Max Weber's image of the "iron cage of bondage" of the modern bureaucratized state. Individual escape routes have been sought by many already. Drugs, crime and suicide, are the destructive side of a pattern that also includes withdrawal to a new privacy. But since the mid-1970s, such anger has found political expression as well. To be precise, it has found two kinds of political expression. It is tempting, though also misleading, to identify these with the right and the left of the political spectrum. In any case, these two trends have altered the agenda of politics in Europe.

There is, first, the new conservatism à l'américain. In essence this is the view that in order to break out of the (social democratic?) cage of bondage, every effort has to be made to stimulate the spirit of enterprise and achievement in people. If in the process some of the traditional values (variously called Victorian or the world of our grandparents or whatever), can be reconstituted, so much the better. Nowhere is this new conservatism quite as influential as in Great Britain, where a specific situation of the Conservative Party, plus the vagaries of the electoral system, have made it possible for Thatcher to become Prime Minister from a clear minority position. The 1982 papers by Albrecht and Lambsdorff on the subect were influential but did not and do not dominate West German politics.[11] In Scandinavia and in the Netherlands, a number of new conservative politicians have risen to positions of power. To some extent, Jacques Chirac is riding on this wave in France. Traces of the view can be found almost anywhere.

There is a variant of this position that is more readily accepted by non-conservatives as well; it is the technological hope. Its central tenet is that unless Europe concentrates its strength on the march into the information society, it will be lost; but if it does so, its future will be safe. Some new conservatives try to combine their Darwinism with technocracy, though this is not easy. The Minister President of the most successful West German state, Lothar Späth of Baden-Württemberg, has made it clear in a recent book that the realization of technological aspirations requires government action and cooperation with big business more than reliance on the market.[12] It appears that in France after the initial phase of traditional socialism, Mitter-

---

[11]Ernst Albrecht, "Zehn Thesen zum Problem der Arbeitslösigkeit," and Otto Graf Lambsdorff, "Konzept für eine Politik zur Überwindung der Wachstumsschwäche und zur Bekämpfung der Arbeitslösigkeit"; both of these important papers and a discussion of their impact after two years can be found in the journal *Liberal,* Konigswinter, 1984, no. 4.

[12]Lothar Späth, *Wende in die Zukunft,* Hamburg: Rowohlt, 1985.

rand's governments have begun to pin their hopes on technology in this sense. Again, traces of the view can be found almost anywhere.

In the context of this essay, the implications of these views for foreign policy attitudes are particularly important. They are also blurred. On the one hand, both the social Darwinist and the technological school of political thought strike a chord in the United States. They borrow American ideas and refer to American experiences as a model. On the other hand, both these views are often coupled with a European brand of "new patriotism" that tends to set Europe, or even particular countries of Europe, against the United States. Thatcher is popular in the United States—but is she an Atlanticist? French technocrats seem quite close to Americans in their way of thinking—but are they really intent on promoting the Alliance? Or does the new conservatism in all its brands espouse an international Darwinism as well, including the deliberate attempt to hold one's own against the great ally across the Atlantic? There are litmus tests for those questions, such as attitudes toward GATT and the European Community, toward the Strategic Defense Initiative and the European Research Cooperation Agency (EUREKA).

The questions are important above all because the other type of political action expressing the anger of the late 1970s is clearly alien to the values of the Alliance. It is that of the protest movements. These include the "peace movement," anti-nuclear groups of many kinds, the Greens, advocates of alternative life styles, and others who try to cash in on doubts about the legitimacy of political regimes, or perhaps about the social democratic consensus. They all have friends in the United States whom they like to quote; they even dream of a "rainbow coalition" of their own; but their views dissociate their movements in two important respects from the American experience. They are skeptics, if not outright opponents of NATO and all that it stands for, and their view of society is different from that of the Western industrial tradition.

Neither of these postures is unambiguous or even clear, and it would be wrong to try to put the protest movements into convenient boxes of good and evil. Their members are often more sincere than sophisticated and find it difficult to distinguish between pacifism, unilateralism, neutralism, and the mere advocacy of disarmament talks and nonproliferation. But they tend to blame either America, or at least "the two superpowers" (a notion they have managed to introduce into everyday language) for the nuclear worry that motivates much of their action. In any case, the Alliance as a guarantee of peace and liberty does not figure in their views.

This is of course closely related to a tendency on the part of the protest movements to denigrate the values by which Western economies and societies have lived since the war. Again, there are many conflicting viewpoints among the movements, and it would be wrong to call the protesters simply socialists, let alone communists. They point to "mass unemployment" as an indictment of our societies; but whereas some demand an even further extension of the public sector ("employment creation"), others advocate individual paths out of the present situation into an "alternative" economy; and there are those who want both. They defend and resent the social state at the same time, because they want security but dislike bureaucracy. They waver between advocating no growth and demanding qualitative growth. One might be tempted to turn Richard Hofstadter's dictum about the (new) conservatives around and say about the protesters: we may wonder whether, in the entire history of thought, there was ever a progressive stance so utterly conservative as this. But then one remembers the ominous world of German cultural pessimists around the turn of the century that Fritz Stern has described so hauntingly in his *Politics of Cultural Despair*.[13]

Such are the views of the new groups that have influenced the agenda of European politics in the last ten years. The broad center has maintained its majority but lost its intellectual and political momentum. New challenges have come from the Darwinists, the technocrats, the protesters. But how strong are they? Are they really the future? Who are they anyway? Here, we must take up the thread of the story where we left it in discussing postwar Europe.

The social democratic consensus had its heyday after 1968, or

---

[13]Fritz Stern, *The Politics of Cultural Despair: A Study in the Rise of the Germanic Ideology,* Berkeley: University of California Press, 1961.

perhaps, after "1968." For a brief moment in history, all major political parties in most European countries espoused much the same position. To all of them however, the 1970s came as a shock. While their immediate reaction was to try to tinker with the system in order to adapt it, they soon realized that this was not enough. Stagflation was just a foretaste of things to come. The three major problems referred to above pose more serious challenges. If the social state cannot be sustained, then one of the pillars of generalized citizenship rights falls. If unemployment becomes a more than conjunctural phenomenon, and a new underclass of marginalized individuals emerges, then the assumptions of the work society may have to be reexamined. All of a sudden there are threats to law and order in a fundamental sense, not just because the number of muggings and burglaries may have grown. The question arises—a very European question perhaps, but nonetheless a real one—what holds these advanced societies together. Such a question has ramifications, including the perception of Europe held by the great ally across the Atlantic. At some point around 1980, a little earlier in some countries and a little later in others, there occurred what in the Federal Republic has been given the name, *Wende*.[14] A reversal of trends set in, or at any rate a gradual turning of the tide. In some cases, governments changed, in others, they merely changed policy. But everywhere, a new mood of restraint and doubt became a point of departure for two major new concerns. One was, and is, the agonizing reappraisal of the welfare state. In politics, such reappraisals are rarely systematic; they consist of the response to exigencies rather than of new designs; still, social policy is being transformed all over Europe. A new balance of the individual and the state is sought everywhere. The other new concern has to do with the search for innovation. Some, notably in France, bank on the technological hope; others, notably in Great Britain, on that of supply-side economics. No one has so far been spectacularly successful, least of all the government that invented the word, *Wende*. Most have done little more than re-

---

[14]The word was probably invented by Hans-Dietrich Genscher in a letter to members of the Free Democratic Party in the autumn of 1982. It alludes to the earlier notion, *Tendenzwende* or reversal of trends; see the book published under this title by Ernst Klett Verlag, Stuttgart, 1975.

duce increases in public spending and improve the tax position of the better-to-do. However, the direction of things has changed.

The late 1970s were a time of quite startling political changes. Thatcher's election in 1979 is but one example. The Scandinavian countries (other than Finland) and Holland offer others, as do, in their ways, France and Spain, and even West Germany where the real *Wende* occurred when Helmut Schmidt took the reins of power from Willy Brandt. In the 1980s, governments appear to be more stable. Some were actually reelected. All have continued along a line that may be described as social democratic tempered by elements of new conservatism. Perhaps it is a safe bet that in domestic affairs this will be the prevailing political mood of Europe for some time to come. It is supported by the alliance of those who live on public money and at least some of those who are impatient with the stagnation of the 1960s. This majority is hard to beat.

But there is an opposition, and its effect on the political agenda is more problematic. Perhaps, the Greens in West Germany tell the story for more than one country. When they decided to channel a widespread protest mood into the straitjacket of a political party, they embarked on a journey that disillusioned socialists like Robert Michels had described many decades earlier.[15] How were they to escape the "iron law of oligarchy"—that is, the rule that all organizations develop their hierarchies and separate power centers? They did not, although they tried, by "rotating" their members of parliament, involving their total membership whenever possible ("basis democracy"), and continuing to seek relations with extraparliamentary protest groups. None of this helped. As a party, they were doomed to remain an episode. They are, of course, by their nature, episodic. There is no coherent "rainbow" platform that effectively links ecologists, unilateralists, feminists and those many others who would like to see their specific causes generalized. But the more important point is that, having created a party to fight all parties, they dis-

---

[15]See Robert Michels, *Soziologie des Parteiwesens: Untersuchungen uber die ologarchischen Tendenzen des Gruppenlebens*, Stuttgart: Kroner, 1925.

cover they are subject to the inertia, the limitations, the frustrations of all parties.

The Greens as a party will thus probably disappear before long. But they will leave their imprint. One will be a growing inclination for situational politics, for mass demonstrations, for more or less spontaneous reactions to specific policy measures, for civil disobedience. Another mark the Greens will leave is even more important. They have helped shift traditional center-left parties away from the center. Electoral interest; the attraction of new ideas; the curious political stance of the "1968"ers; the public service class, notably teachers, social workers and the like—all have combined to lead Social Democrats away from the social democratic consensus. In domestic affairs, this shift probably has limited impact. Radicalized Social Democrats have few genuine alternatives to offer, and when they get into power, they soon find themselves constrained by conditions beyond their control. In international affairs, the shift is more serious. It is not entirely absurd to surmise that in large parts of Europe, we are entering a phase in which the domestic mix of social democracy and new conservatism will be combined with a certain coolness toward the Atlantic Alliance.

Parties of the traditional left have shifted further in Protestant Europe than in Catholic Europe; indeed it could be argued that the new protest movements are largely a Protestant phenomenon. Thus, there are variations of the degree of coolness exhibited toward the Alliance. But everywhere a position is gaining ground that argues roughly as follows: the overriding concern of international politics in peace. The two superpowers are engaged in actions that threaten peace rather than promote it. In their respective spheres of interest, they pursue traditional power politics (Afghanistan, Central America). In relations with each other, they have allowed themselves to be dragged into an arms race without limits. Europeans must not only put pressure on the superpowers to return to the negotiating table but must also stay out of the vicious circle themselves. This will mean a reduction and eventual removal of (non European?) nuclear weapons from Europe, and the active exploration of Europe's own capacity for defense.

There are variations on this theme, notably in relation to nuclear weapons. Also, it is generally asserted that "the two super-powers" are, of course, very different. Moreover, some are strongly opposed to such positions, including prominent social democrats like Helmut Schmidt and Britain's Social Democratic Party co-founder David Owen, to say nothing of Latin Socialists like François Mitterrand, Spain's Prime Minister Felipe González and Italy's Prime Minister Bettino Craxi. But this cannot detract from the importance of the shift of the European left in matters of international policy. What is more, many who are not supporters of the left would find their views plausible. Assessing the significance and the practical effect of such trends is perhaps the key to an understanding of Europe and the Alliance.

Which Europe?

When Konrad Adenauer firmly linked the Federal Republic of Germany to the West, his tactical mind and his deeper inclinations were at one. He knew of course that given the world scene after the breakup of the wartime alliance, only an unambiguous commitment to one side would enable him, and the Federal Republic, to find a respected place in the concert of nations. But beyond that, his heart had always led him to the West. It is said that when Adenauer, as the Mayor of Cologne from 1917 to 1920 and as President of the Prussian State Council in the 1920s, had to go to Berlin, he invariably felt a certain hesitation about crossing the river Elbe eastward. Adenauer had his disappointments, notably in Europe; but when he finally resigned as chancellor in 1963, he had achieved what one might call (if the metaphor is not too misleading in this context), the Russian doll effect: open up the Atlantic Alliance and out comes the European Community; open up the European Community and out comes Franco-German cooperation; open up Franco-German cooperation and out comes the Federal Republic of Germany. German interest, friendship across the Rhine, West European integration, and the all-encompassing Alliance fit neatly into each other, or so it seemed.

The early opposition to Adenauer's concept had two spokesmen, the SPD and the Free Democratic Party, but one theme. It was reunification. Whereas Adenauer argued that the distant objective of German reunification could be attained only from a position of Western solidarity and strength, the opposition warned that every step toward integrating Germany into the West would make reunification that much more unlikely. Adenauer eventually won the day. Even though both the SPD and FDP voted against the Treaty of Paris (which created the European Coal and Steel Community in 1952), by the time the ratification debate for the Treaty of Rome (which set up the European Economic Community in 1958) took place, the FDP had come around to Adenauer's view. The SPD continued to be opposed, but three years later it too made its peace with what might well be called the *raison d'état* of the Federal Republic of Germany.

This is a long story cut very short indeed. It leaves out divisions within all political parties as well as the saga of Stalin's 1952 note proposing the withdrawal of all foreign troops and a neutral, reunited Germany, the debacle of the European Defense Community, and above all those unforgotten milestones of the history of liberty in postwar Europe—East Germany in 1953, Hungary in 1956, to which later were added Czechoslovakia in 1968 and Poland in 1980. In the end, it was less Adenauer's will than the Soviet threat that brought about the West German foreign policy consensus. On a more mundane level, one may have to add the economic success of the Federal Republic, which detracted attention from the great national and international issues.

At least it did for a while. Whether by historical accident or not, the phase of domestic reform—i.e., the second half of the 1960s—was also a time of reappraisal of West Germany's foreign policy. Then-Chancellor Kurt-Georg Kiesinger's earliest statements seemed to open doors in a new direction; as foreign minister of Kiesinger's "grand coalition," Willy Brandt and his chief of planning, Egon Bahr, mapped the route to take once one had walked through these doors. This is what came to be called, after Brandt himself had become Chancellor in 1969, *Ostpolitik,* or rather *Ost-und Deutschlandpolitik*—the Federal Republic's policy with respect to Eastern Europe and the two German states. The stages of implementation of this policy were as hotly contested as Adenauer's *Westpolitik,* although once again the conflict ended in a broad consensus of views. In the end, another Russian doll emerged beginning with *détente,* or more specifically, the Helsinki process, containing within it a more relaxed relationship between countries of Western and Eastern Europe, but above all a new active partnership between the two Germanies.

All this was of course conceived as a necessary supplement and not as a substitute for the Western Alliance. But the curious fact remains that the motivation for the new departure has never been very clear. Not that anyone tried to conceal it; the actors simply did not make it explicit even to themselves. Probably, Brandt genuinely felt that "normalization" was imperative in relations with Eastern Europe. His kneeling down at the Warsaw ghetto monument was as symbolic for his motives (and his spontaneity) as the mass in the cathedral of Reims with Charles de Gaulle was for Adenauer's (and his tactical genius). Walter Schleel on the other hand, foreign minister under Brandt, wanted above all to extend West Germany's international room for maneuver, not least in the West, by removing possible instruments of blackmail by others. For him, *Ostpolitik* involved merely a set of calculated sacrifices. Again, Bahr may well have had wider designs. He may have thought—as some think to the present day—that it is West Germany's manifest destiny to seek conditions in Europe that bring the German states closer together. Throughout, there was a great deal of quite un-German pragmatism. Yet the opaqueness of motives leaves much room for interpretation at home and abroad, misinterpretation not excluded.

However, this is not the point of the story. The point is not at all local, let alone parochial. It is rather that the Alliance is not all there is to the foreign policy of the countries of Europe. This is commonplace, but it needs emphasis. There are historical, geopolitical, economic, cultural and probably other interests that complicate the neat fit of the original Russian doll. If there is any reality to the observation of a growing Europeanization of Europe, it has something to do with the relative importance of these interests.

The German question is, of course, itself one key to the European question. Contrary to a whole lot of other pending issues, it has never been a question for just one country and perhaps one or two of its neighbors; it has long reverberated across the whole of Europe and will continue to do so. The prevailing (though not the only) West German view on this question is shared by this author. It is, in the words of West German President Richard von Weizsäcker, that the German question remains open as long as a wall blocks the Brandenburg Gate and divides Berlin and Germany but that the answer is not reunification in traditional national terms. Rather the answer lies in the creation of conditions in the whole of Europe by which borders lose their divisiveness, so that bridges can be built between separate states and countries. The two Germanies can only move closer together in the context of a European regime of peace.

This is foreign policy language and may sound imprecise and therefore suspicious. However, what it means is quite clear and very important. So far as German policy is concerned, it means three simple things. The first is that as a practical political objective national reunification is not on the German agenda. The second is that peaceful and developing relations with the part of Europe to which the other Germany belongs is one major motive of West German policy. The third is that the improvement of direct relations with the German Democratic Republic, while confined to relatively minor matters in view of the difference in social and political systems, has a high priority for the Federal Republic. And all this must not detract from membership in the Atlantic Alliance.

This is where the most complicated issues of mutual support and understanding commence. For one thread of the argument of this essay concerns a dilemma of trans-Atlantic relations that the German case makes painfully obvious. The Europeanization of Europe complicates matters, but the Americanization of America tends toward simplicity. As the interests of European countries, and of that nebulous yet real entity, Europe, become more explicit, there is, if anything, less readiness in the United States to bear with complexity. The result is unfortunate. In the United States there is a growing feeling that Europe may be drifting away from the Alliance, and in Europe there is a corresponding feeling that one can achieve one's proper objectives only apart from, if not against, the United States. Perhaps one should not exaggerate the importance of either. There is little doubt in Europe about the role of America, and about its inner strength as well as international power, and some appearances notwithstanding, Americans, including their leaders, still have a very special place for Europeans in their hearts and minds. But clearly, Europe's hesitant search for a complex identity, and America's confident assertion of strength, leave room for many a misunderstanding. The German question is one of the causes.

To return to Europe, Germany is of course by no means the only country with its own deep historical interests. In fact, the concerns of some others are in conflict with those of Germany. French (and in other ways Polish) policy is at least in part motivated by the desire to prevent the reemergence of a Germany that upsets the postwar balance of impotence. (One must never forget that this is a deep-seated Soviet motive as well.) For this reason as well as for more benevolent reasons of history, French relations with some of the smaller countries of Eastern Europe have traditionally been strong. Great Britain has been torn since the war between a fading yet important Commonwealth, an abstract yet widely acknowledged special relationship with the United States, and an unwanted yet imperative European destiny. For a long time, Italy, Holland, Belgium and Luxembourg have found it easier than others to support unambiguously both West European integration and the Atlantic Alliance.

There is no point in recounting the obvious, which is that Europe signifies difference, so that any generalization is as much a statement about the author's perspective as about the real world. Clearly, this essay is written by a German who has had some exposure to Great Britain and to the European Community, but whose knowledge of other corners of the old continent is much less intimate. However, it is hard to think of a European perspective that does not include a reference to the issue of diversity and unity itself.

The return of fundamentalism is not just characteristic of the Islamic world. Elsewhere, and in the West as well, there is also a desire to substitute simple sentiments for the effort of comprehension. In such circumstances, Europe goes against the prevailing trend and must do so. Europe is a complex entity, and

Europeans have learned to live with complexity. It would be contrary to West Germany's interest to seek neutrality, and contrary to France's or Great Britain's tradition to do so, but Swiss or Austrian or Swedish neutrality does not shock Europeans. They are also different versions of the same concept. The terrible word, "Finlandization," is occasionally used by Europeans too, but most know that Finland is a free country, the international position of which is constrained by certain unavoidable but bearable limitations. Romania, Hungary, Czechoslovakia and Poland are all communist countries, but they are at least as different in culture and society, domestic and international outlook as any four West European countries.

And they are all European. Nowhere is the word, Europe, used with more commitment than in Eastern Europe. Poland has even made sure that it remains in the same time zone as the rest of the continent, so that two hours separate Warsaw time from Moscow time. All other Europeans resent it if members of the European Community refer to themselves as Europe, as if the accident of organization could override the wide and deeper reality. Naturally, there are doubts at the margin. Will Turkey remain a European country? Does Iceland belong? Are the countries of the southern Mediterranean really African rather than European? But in a significant sense, the European Community and the members of the Council of Europe, the Nordic countries and the Balkan countries, the countries of the Baltic and of the Danube—overlapping as many of them are—are all part of Europe. They figure not only in sporting events in which European Cups can be won, or in the Conference on Security and Cooperation in Europe, but also in the national perceptions and policies of every one of them.

And the Soviet Union? There are two questions here. One is whether the Soviet Union belongs to that elusive yet influential entity called Europe. Soviet sportsmen and women compete for European Cups; the U.S.S.R. was obviously a part of the Helsinki process. But that is not the point. Nor is geography, although de Gaulle's "Europe from the Atlantic to the Urals" clearly leaves an interesting ambiguity in this respect. In terms of the notion of Europe underlying this argument, and probably the one that is relevant for policymakers, the Soviet Union does not belong The reason is that Europe is perceived as consisting of small and medium-sized countries. It does not include a superpower, nor does it aspire to be one. Whatever Russia's role in the history and culture of Europe may be, the Soviet Union represents ambitions and instruments of domination that are alien to Europe today.

From an Alliance point of view, another facet of the question may seem more pressing. How can one discuss Europe without placing much greater emphasis on the Soviet threat and the fundamental difference of social and political systems that divides the continent? Does not the very notion of Europe advanced here betray a fundamental weakness of analysis, if not of attitude? Is not in fact the only Europe of interest the set of free countries willing to defend themselves against communist imperialism? There are those, in Europe as well as in the United States, who think so. However, a majority of policymakers, and of ordinary people, have a somewhat more complicated image of Europe, East and West. This can be described without recourse to dubious speculation about motives in the Kremlin or anywhere else. The description answers at the time the question of which Europe we are talking about when we refer to the Europeanization of Europe.

There are different social and political systems in Europe. People have long decided with their feet which they prefer. Given the choice, all Europeans would prefer variants of the Western rather than the Eastern system. Conditions of power, and above all the geopolitical interests of the Soviet Union, prevent East Europeans from having and doing what they want. The result is an inherently unstable situation. While this is interpreted differently by different groups, and not everyone likes to draw the conclusions suggested here, there is wide consensus on an analysis along the following lines. The East European situation is domestically unstable, as the growing list of protests all the way to abortive revolutions shows. It is therefore a source of concern for the Soviet Union that leads to international instability. Apart from its ideological claims to supremacy and what they may or may not mean, the Soviet Union must be assumed to be worried about those whose way of life has a certain magnetic force for people in its own orbit. At the very least, the

Soviet Union has an interest in neutralizing this magnetism; given certain conditions, it may be tempted to attack the source of that magnetism with force. In this sense, there is a Soviet threat and a need for defense. The need cannot be satisfied by Europeans alone. Advanced defense technology on the super-power level exceeds European capabilities, and in any case, European conflicts would have ramifications far beyond Europe's borders. Thus, the defense of free Europe has to be Atlantic rather than just European. We need the Alliance to be safe.

However, European security cannot be built on arms alone. If this is tried it will turn the necessary tools of defense into possible threats to peace. This is why defense and détente are, and have to remain, complementary elements of a security policy in Europe. *Détente* means more than being nice to each other (although style is not to be underrated). It means the systematic removal at least of those sources of conflict that do not touch on the essential difference between the systems. Guaranteed borders are one case in point. Open information in many areas is another. Trade can be both of interest in itself and a vehicle for other contacts. Numerous specific and wider issues of this kind have been identified in the Helsinki process. This then leaves the more sensitive areas of East-West relations. These are not products listed somewhere as proscribed for trade; truly sensitive areas for different systems always concern people and ideas. This is why active *détente* is about mobility—that is, emigration, travel, tourism—about scientific and cultural cooperation, and in the end, even about the common adherence to certain values, such as basic human rights. The approach needed here is difficult precisely because the issues are sensitive. Free people detest a system in which elementary rights are violated. Presumably, at least the communist *nomenklatura* dislikes the very openness of Western systems of which we are justly proud. There is no reason whatever why clear language should not be used in mutual relations so that there is not even a hint of appeasement in the intention of *détente*. But there remains a case for cooperation. Sensitive issues should be dealt with in a spirit of mutual respect. Such issues should be viewed as an opportunity to find mutually acceptable solutions rather than as a way to fight war with other means.

All this requires steady nerves and a clear sense of direction. It also requires a very special confidence within the Alliance. The European view is that effective defense, in the sense of preparedness and of discouragement of attack, is necessary. But the European view is not and cannot be that a line between the kingdom of "evil" and of "good" divides Berlin, Germany and Europe as a whole. There is too much history to link the various parts of Europe. This includes large parts of what is now the Soviet Union. There are too many relations across the divide, from television through travel to trade and cultural cooperation and of course the European Cups in sports. There is too much awareness of the varieties of development in different countries, including the varieties of communism. There are too many interests that the small and medium-sized countries of Europe share. A very special kind of confidence within the Alliance means therefore that Americans in particular must appreciate that there is no contradiction between the unambiguous preparedness to defend liberty and the acceptance of the complexity which is Europe.

A Possible European Community

Despite what has been said, there is a growing tendency in everyday language, both across the Atlantic and on its Eastern side, to say Europe when one means the European Community. This is understandable. People would like to put their finger on this vexing entity, and the only tangible organization of things European that stands, however shakily, among the ruins of attempts at organization is the EC in Brussels. (Or is it Strasbourg, or even Luxembourg?) The Organization for European Economic Cooperation long ago became the Organization for Economic Cooperation and Development. The Council of Europe, while still important, is reduced to issues like human rights and cultural cooperation. The European Defense Community never came off, and European Union is still a dream. The Conference on Security and Cooperation is a process rather than an organization. So when all is said and done one invariably comes back to the European Communities (as their precise name has been since the merger of the original communities in 1967),[16] which at least have buildings, a legal base, a commission, a council of ministers, a court of law and many other prerequisites for real existence.

This is all to the good because the history of the EC is one of an irritating conflict between aspiration and reality. It has always claimed to be so much more than it is that it was bound to mislead not only outsiders but insiders as well. On the one hand, it has behaved as if it was a kind of European government; the red carpet was rolled out for visiting dignitaries by the first Commission President Walter Hallstein, and more recently, the Commission president has come to join the "Big Seven" at their annual economic summits. On the other hand, the institutions of Brussels look desperately like an extremely costly mechanism to protect European agriculture; two-thirds or more of the budget is spent on this sector. For a while, there were those ("functionalists") who believed that there was a "necessary" process to close the gap between ambition and fact. "Economic and Monetary Union" was the link for them. Since its failure in the often-cited storms of the early 1970s, a different approach has gained ground. But it is still difficult to make statements about the EC that are not blurred either by unfounded idealism or by unnecessary cynicism. Yet it is important to recognize the achievements and failures of the European Community if one wants to understand the Europeanization of Europe and its impact on the Alliance.

One way of describing the EC is by these efforts or attempts to close the gap between aspiration and reality. So far, they have all failed to a greater or lesser extent. But it is characteristic and significant that every attempt has left certain traces, which are real enough, and moreover that there is always a new impetus for trying again. Europe lives, if only by trial and error.

The first attempt at European unification (leaving the long prehistory of the idea to one side) was a part of the postwar reconstruction. Its aspirations were defined in all their splendor

---

[16]The European Coal and Steel Community, the European Atomic Community, and the European Economic Community.

and ambiguity by Winston Churchill in his famous speeches of 1945 and 1946. Centuries of "civil war" in Europe had to come to an end. Europe had to find itself as one actor in the world. Was Great Britain to be a part of it? Or a benevolent bystander? Or perhaps the great mediator between a United Europe and the United States of America, in a kind of double special relationship? In any case, there was no contradiction between the European dream and the reality of the emerging Atlantic Alliance. What remained of the dream, may seem little, but it is important. It was the European Coal and Steel Community, with its far-reaching institutional arrangements, the brainchild of its first president, the great Jean Monnet. Coal and steel were at the time anything but declining industries. Nevertheless, the limitations of the first community also betrayed the fact that when it comes to implementing dreams, interests matter above all. France's interest in containing West Germany was as important as West Germany's interest in returning to the fold. Thus in a sense the mountain, after all the rolling thunder of integration, gave birth to a mouse; but the new reality was there to stay.

The second attempt at European unification arose from the ashes of the European Defense Community. If defense was not to be the great federator, could it be economic cooperation? This was still the Europe of Adenauer and Robert Schuman, Alcide de Gasperi and Paul-Henri Spaak; before long, of Hallstein and Sicco Mansholt, and of course the shadow and soon again the reality, of de Gaulle. But once more the result, the European Economic Community (and the more modest European Atomic Community), which began work in 1958, fell far short of the dreams of the founders. In essence, it amounted to three things, a commitment to trade liberalization, an ever bigger program to cushion the decline of the agricultural population, and a set of institutions that could be regarded as the nucleus of a future government rather than as a secretariat. Once again, interest prevailed, French interest in particular. The United States could afford to take a benevolent view of this new creation. This was of course the time of shared interests, especially in the Kennedy Round. Within Europe, West Germany, but also Italy and the Benelux countries, saw to it that the more divisive attempts by France to draw a sharp line between Europe and the United

States were not allowed to dominate.

Possibly the most important aspect of the European Economic Community (EEC) was that it was defined as a process. The common market was to be created in stages. This meant that there was a definable program of action, especially if one ventured into the unlimited field of non-tariff barriers. By 1969, however, this process came to an end. Once again, objectives had to be redefined. The European summit at The Hague in December 1969 marked the beginning of the third attempt at European integration. The acts were a new generation, France's President Georges Pompidou, Chancellor Brandt, before long Britain's Prime Minister Edward Heath, and a European Commission that stretched from the last of the first Europeans, Sicco Mansholt and Altiero Spinelli, to the first of the new Europeans, Raymond Barre, for example. The theme for the years to come was defined by the French triptych, *achévement, élargissement, appronfondissement.*

Achévement meant the completion of the program of the original EEC, the common market. In a technical sense, this was achieved in the spring of 1970. Technicalities apart, there emerged the reality of Brussels as it still is today, the very reality that is the subject of so much criticism, cynicism and caricature at home and abroad. Its main elements are these: the European Community administers, guards, and to a lesser extent develops an imperfect common market for industrial products that provides member countries with advantages of free trade above and beyond those of the GATT. The EC protects certain declining industries, notably agriculture, but also steel and certain other industries where international agreements regulate trade. Such protection has many forms, especially in agriculture where a common policy is jointly financed to the tune of more than $40 billion per year. The EC takes a special interest in a large number of developing countries, former colonies of member states, by offering them trade advantages, a certain stabilization of export earnings, some aid, and a certain amount of technical cooperation. The EC effects a relatively minor transfer of resources from advantaged to disadvantaged regions and social groups within Europe. It finances and coordinates the financing of research, especially in areas related to nuclear energy, but also in other fields of high technology. The EC produces reports and proposals in many other policy realms that may or may not be adopted by member states. This is clearly not negligible, though if the various elements are given the weight that they have been given by the member states, there is a somewhat unfortunate prevalence toward protecting declining sectors of the economy.

The second part of the 1969 triptych, *élargissement*, was on the face of it, also the most successful. The original community had six members, West Germany, France, Italy, Belgium, the Netherlands and Luxembourg. From the beginning, the principle of equal status was crucial for the community; this is one aspect of the specifically European nature of the construction. In 1973 Great Britain, Ireland and Denmark joined (though Norway did not since the accession treaty was rejected in a referendum). Eight years later, Greece followed suit, and by 1986, the accession of Spain and Portugal will mean that 12 countries belong to the EC. The enlargement of the European Community is not just a quantitative success. It indicates that the EC continues to be attractive for the (more or less) developed democratic countries of Europe, and must increasingly be regarded as their spokesman. But enlargement also had a high price, not just because of Spanish olives, the British rebate or Greece's Mediterranean predilections. In a larger community, especially one that does not include some obvious candidates (like Sweden and Norway, Switzerland and Austria), the area of common or even overlapping interest dwindles. It is bound to do so, even if one discounts idiosyncracy. Marginal motives play an inordinate part; there is frustration about more central ones. The familiar conflict between aspiration and reality turns into one between different aspirations.

This is above all relevant for the least successful, but most important element of the triptych, *approfondissement*. This extension, or intensification, of community in Europe had one name, economic and monetary union. It was in fact an attempt to set in motion another process analogous to the creation of the common market. Within ten years and in three stages full monetary union was supposed to be achieved, including of course the coordination and eventual integration of economic policy and the development of supporting policies in the regional and social fields. Once again, the "functionalists" hoped they had found a master key to unification, a method that would make it all but inevitable. It was to be the last time that such hopes had any chance at all. The project of economic and monetary union turned out to be a dismal failure. Within weeks of the decision by the Council of Ministers to enter the first stage of the process in the spring of 1971, floating started and destroyed any prospect of a European laboratory experiment. A few attempts were made to rescue rudiments of the project; this was the time of the "tunnel" and of the "snake" in the tunnel—that is, of narrower exchange-rate bands for European currencies than those that emerged in relation to the dollar. But within a year or so, economic and monetary union as a project was dead.

Rarely has a failure been more beneficial than this one. It turned Europe from an experiment into a reality. Once again, collapse did not quell the motive to go forward. But from that point on, going forward no longer meant grand designs. The European Community had at last learned that it could not impose its own calendar on a recalcitrant reality but had to conduct its affairs like everyone else, by a combination of policy objectives and responses to circumstances. In fact, this is what happened in subsequent years. The result may displease institutional purists, but at least it is real, because it is based on interest. The European Monetary System, which was set up by some, though not all, members of the EC, may be a modest arrangement, but it has helped its members deal better with some of the pressures on currencies in recent years. Also, and despite the continuing skepticism of the West German Federal Bank, the creation of a European currency unit, the ECU, may yet turn out to have wider significance. Other initiatives were often taken in the same manner, *à la carte*—that is, they involved only those who showed an interest. From the Airbus to Ariane, from ESPRIT to EUREKA, there are now some important joint technological ventures in Europe. In virtually all fields of policy, intergovernmental cooperation has increased. Moreover, there is a directly elected European Parliament.

And there is institutional cooperation in foreign policy. This actually stems from the 1969 Hague summit and the creation of a system of a Political Committee shortly thereafter that holds regular meetings of the political directors of foreign ministries and of the ministers themselves. The results are, as a rule, not formal decisions. But political cooperation exemplifies two other achievements of the European Community in recent years that are often not understood outside, or even inside, the EC. The first is the development of what Andrew Shonfield called the "habit of cooperation."[17] This should not be underrated. Politicians in and out of government, officials, representatives of interests of many kinds now find it easy and normal to talk to their opposite numbers in other EC countries. A network of contacts has been created that is as real as the national institutions through which people act. The habit of cooperation does not, of course, mean agreement, let alone binding decisions, but it does mean an increasing community of substance.

This is where a second achievement should be noted. It is that Europe—the European Community—even now may not often speak with one voice, but its several voices may in fact say much the same thing. As the habit of cooperation grows, several things happen. People listen, take the views of others into account, reexamine their own, and almost inevitably adjust them. People also discover those common conditions that bind them together and sometimes even the interests that take them forward together. The result does not sound terribly *communautaire*. Politicians and officials in particular still like to couch their interests in the language to which they are accustomed and resist attempts to abandon their local traditions in favor of one voice. This is exasperating for outsiders who cannot easily tell what is behind the different voices, let alone who decided what. It is nevertheless one way for Europe to move ahead. For, without handing over sovereignty and creating a European Union, Europeans have in fact come to think and act in similar ways.

If this sounds vague, it may help to add that it is an attempt to describe relations between Europe and the United States. Perhaps it should be emphasized that the description betrays the European angle from which it is attempted. The third phase of

---

[17]Andrew Shonfield, *Europe: Journey to an Unknown Destination*, London: Allen Lane, 1973.

European unification of which we are still speaking was also one of increasingly uneasy trans-Atlantic relations. At the surface this unease had to do with certain irritants—agricultural protectionism and proscribed technology, shoes, soybeans and spaghetti. Somewhat deeper down a curious symbolic debate began about how to conduct relations. "Diplomatic" relations were established between the United States and the EC; there was much talk of a regular dialogue and some reality to it; there was even a Year of Europe. But all this was symbolic. If relations are easy, one does not need to debate institutions. In the 1950s and 1960s, a Year of Europe would have seemed very strange. Thus one is led once again to those underlying changes of posture, and perhaps of interest, that have been one of the threads running through the argument of this essay.

The initial motive forces of European cooperation and integration came from several sources. There was an emergent international condition that required as much cooperation as possible to defend freedom in the West. There was the deep-seated desire to put an end to what was at last perceived to be civil war in Europe. There were the specific interests of France and West Germany, and the possibility of striking a bargain between them. All these converged in the postwar years, and they all were not only tolerable for the United States but invited active support. They fitted into the Alliance and also into the kind of world order that had arisen from the ashes of the war. More recently, these rudiments of a world order have crumbled. We have retold a part of the story earlier. There has been a return to a cruder exercise of power and thus, in Europe, a more acute sense of impotence. The process has been accompanied by the halting yet unmistakable assertion of particular interests, and more, of peculiar socio-economies and socio-political traditions on either side of the Atlantic. America's "flexible flexibility" produces both envy and fear in Europe; Europe's "rigid flexibility" calls forth the disdain but also the respect of Americans. All this does not mean that European integration at this stage is directed against the United States, but it does mean that one of its motives is the assertion of difference, of a European way forward.

This involves a difficult transition. It has been described as one from a partnership between a senior and a junior partner to one of more nearly equal partners. Such imagery has its value, but it also has limitations. Clearly, the American position in defense terms remains, and will remain, one of domination even if Europe's contribution should become more visible. American political influence, while not simply a function of military superiority, is and will be incomparably greater all over the world than that of Europe. In economic terms too, American interest rates, or indebtedness, will continue to have a greater impact on the rest of the world than corresponding developments in Europe would. The ECU is not about to replace the dollar, or even the Eurodollar. If one were to hold against this merely the hope of Europe—even the hope that countries all over the world pin on Europe—one would fall into the old trap of confusing aspiration with reality. But the emergence of a European pattern of economy and society, the insistence of European interests in East-West relations, the traces of a European self-confidence that is not by the same token Atlantic, plus the results of that curious "two steps forward, one step back" progression of attempts at organized European cooperation, add up to an unmistakable picture of change. Partnership is certainly a good word to use; we shall use it again in summarizing the argument. But in substance, the transition in question is above all one from an all-embracing, almost familial relationship to one that is more explicitly contractual, from a family business to a limited liability company.

Leaving metaphors to one side, one question is: How should the United States view these new developments? How should it cope with the fact that so much of it is slow, unstructured and incomplete? Would American support still be welcomed by those who wish to advance a more European Europe, and if so, what form should it take? The answers are no more simple than the description of the process itself. Clearly, the new phase of European cooperation is not as immediately in the American interest as the initial one. Thus, supporting it would itself require a more sophisticated approach. It would also require an appreciation of long-term interests. For Europe and the United States are the two models of prosperity in freedom that the world has to offer. They belong together for this fundamental reason, if for no other. It may well be critical for the world whether both sides appreciate this community without trying to impose their own style on the other.

So far, the new relationship has not been worked out. Indeed, there is a temptation for Europe simply to insist on the power of complexity and for the United States, on the simplicity of power. Perhaps developing a new habit of cooperation across the Atlantic will help. In this respect, the economic summits are undoubtedly useful. But they are not enough. And to return to the story of European integration, the difficulty remains that there is no focus. To whom is one to talk in Europe to negotiate the new relationship across the Atlantic? To the European Commission in Brussels? More than ever, this would risk losing those who really matter. To Bonn, Paris and London? It may be that Europe will move forward in "two speeds" and even that new initiatives will have to come from France and West Germany above all, but nothing would be more counterproductive than any attempt, even unintended, to divide up Europeans and concentrate on the seemingly important ones. There is in fact no choice but to accept that Europe has many voices, though it is necessary also to listen to the similarities of what these voices say.

This is difficult enough to accept for Europeans. Indeed, one can understand those who would prefer to return to the old family relationship of the Alliance. The very least that must be said is that the present phase of European cooperation is less Cartesian than earlier ones. This does not make it any less significant. The institutions of the European Community, what is commonly called, "Brussels," remain important, but they are not likely to become the source of major new developments. These take place at the margin. Sometimes they only involve some of the member states of the European Community, but not others. In some respects they involve non-members; technology and monetary-cooperation are examples. Not all new forms of cooperation are based on binding decisions. Habit, intergovernmental and even nongovernmental agreements, or a mere parallelism of action all play their part. In the process, a great deal of European reality is assembled. Paradoxically perhaps, while its institutions may appear weak, Europe is in fact more real than ever before.

One day this reality will undoubtedly find institutional expression. Some believe that the moment for this fourth great

European initiative has come already. At the June 1985 European Council meeting in Milan, it was decided to convene a conference of member-states before the end of the year in order to agree on steps toward European union. Probably the time is not yet ripe to accomplish very much in this respect. But the attempt shows that the idea of European unity is alive and that a history of apparent failures has in fact yielded a strong base for implementing the idea.

Challenges to the Atlantic Alliance

What does all this add up to when it comes to the future of the Atlantic Alliance? Translating economic, social and even political trends into foreign policy stances is a highly speculative art. Things are rarely as clear as they are in the relationship between fear for one's social and economic position and an inclination toward protectionism rather than open markets; and even in this respect other factors intervene, such as countervailing interests or even the existence of GATT. Generally speaking, the main transmission belts for turning domestic motives into international postures are probably three, public opinion, political parties, and foreign policy elites.

Public opinion in most European countries shows a limited, highly situational interest in foreign policy. Specific events alert the active as well as the normally inactive, especially if they evoke emotions that are latently present at any time. These include the nuclear fear that was activated by the beginning of the deployment of Pershing IIs and cruise missiles in 1983. They also include those fundamental emotions awakened by television pictures of the Ethiopian famine. At a somewhat less elementary level, nationalism, or better perhaps, a sense of national pride continues to be a strong motive (Falkland Islands War, German reunification, French nuclear testing), although there is still a groundswell of feeling in favor of Europe, whatever it means. Without doubt, the image of America has become more blurred at this level; Goethe's *Amerika, du hast es besser,* is now confined to the European view of the domestic scene in the United States. There are many who feel that American life is still as marvelous as ever but that American international attitudes are strangely simplistic, illiberal and aggressive.

Political parties reflect some, though by no means all, of these sentiments. A lively debate about the Alliance, including defense and disarmament, burden-sharing and the place of the United States in the scheme of things, has taken place and continues to take place in almost all European countries in the 1980s. It is full of telling ambiguities. Prime Minister Andreas Papandreou, who once held an American passport, has fueled anti-American sentiment in Greece. Prime Minister González believes in Spain's Western destiny but will try to let a referendum decide on whether his belief prevails. In Norway, all parties share the view that it is best to belong to NATO but reject the more arduous obligations of membership, a view that is not unknown in Denmark, Holland and Belgium. In Great Britain and France, the future of the Alliance is a subject of debate between government and opposition, although there may be more agreement than strikes the eye. French parties are overtly very Atlantic these days; yet few have forgotten the apparently recurrent need for the country either not to practice what it preaches or vice versa. Italy may well be the least ambivalent member of the Alliance. Such a rapid survey shows that we are going to do the almost impossible if we presently try to summarize a few salient points for the whole of Europe.

What then of the foreign policy elites? For one thing, they are unexpectedly small. There have been surprising appointments even to senior government offices in the field. The members of parliamentary committees on foreign affairs cannot always be described as a foreign policy elite. Significant groups have formed around foreign affairs institutes in most countries, but it is doubtful whether their role is more than ancillary when it comes to determining foreign policy. Even in the media, no more than a handful in any country can be described as in-depth analysts of foreign policy. This is important because strong foreign policy elites can add momentum to popular moods or reduce it, and they can influence political parties. To some extent they do, but European foreign policy elites are hardly a major force.

This is not to say of course that there are not certain major directions of political thought and action concerning the Alliance in Europe. Short of technicalities (notably of defense policy), and bearing in mind important variations within and between countries, the following five points are an attempt to summarize Europe's view of the Alliance in the mid-1980s.

First, the continued need for the Atlantic Alliance is unchallenged both in terms of values and of interest. There are those, at the way-out ends of the political spectrum, who disagree; but they are few and far between. There are more, though not among the dominant groups, who like to speculate about a condition in which the Alliance is no longer necessary. Such speculation should not be dismissed lightly. After all, who would not wish to overcome the permanent threat of a bipolar world? But dreams of eternal peace or even of a neutral Europe cannot detract from the realities of power. Even the fact that the Alliance is unloved by many does not affect the sense of necessity that people have. Moreover, this is not just borne out by the kind of analysis presented here. It is also a result of awareness of common values, the shared belief in human rights as well as in social choice, the shared commitment to the open society in which mistakes can be corrected without bloodshed. These values, and their importance for holding the Atlantic Alliance together, are incidentally a strong reason why the Alliance must be seen to be more than a geopolitical exercise.

Second, the physical presence of American forces in Europe remains crucial. Arguments for and against American troops in Europe have been rehearsed many times, especially in the United States. In Europe too, there are those who would prefer the total Europeanization of defense and others who try to play down the importance of an American presence. There are also those few who add force to the case for withdrawal by throwing bombs at American bases. Yet when all historical, symbolic and practical reasons are put to one side, there remains a simple fact. One of the superpowers is very close to Europe; in many ways, it is right in Europe. Insofar as it presents a threat, Europe is clearly one of the theaters where this threat becomes effective. It is therefore crucial that the other great power should be right there too. Balance can be created only if the decoupling of Europe from the Alliance is seen to be impossible. Put differently, America cannot evade the price of its power and be secure itself.

Third, the military posture of the Alliance will get widespread support in Europe only if it is seen to concentrate on minimum effective deterrence. This is as important as it is complicated; and it must be repeated that no technical discussion of defense policy is intended here. One simple way of elaborating on the point is to say that it must at all times be possible to give reasons for what is done. These reasons, moreover, must not consist of experts bandying about dubious figures or uncertain facts about the other side; they must be clear and plausible. Furthermore, it must be evident in the process that it is the unambiguous intention of the Alliance to keep its military potential at the lowest level necessary for effective defense. This includes an indubitable commitment to all measures of mutual and balanced force reduction and of disarmament that can conceivably be achieved. Even the impression that the Western side may not be overly eager to see disarmament talks at whatever level succeed does serious damage to the inner strength of an Alliance based on the values of openness and choice.

Neither the deployment of Pershing IIs and cruise missiles, nor the introduction of the subject of the Strategic Defense Initiative has helped much in this respect. The former left two questions without fully satisfactory answers: Was there not an element of formal equality of numbers rather than minimum effective deterrence in the deployment? Did it not turn, at a certain point, into a show of strength rather than proven need? The latter, SDI, is almost a model of how not to introduce a new idea. An unclear, and perhaps unfinished concept, was accompanied by demands for unquestioned loyalty. To top it all, the atmosphere of discussion became highly charged symbolically. This creates distrust and fear; it should be a lesson.

Fourth, for Europe, *détente* is not dead. It will, on the contrary, remain the other side of defense. Americans rightly ask the question what exactly does *détente* mean. In Europe too, the meaning of the notion is by no means always clear. It is, for example, not easy to see in what sense "a new phase of *détente*" may be beginning in the mid-1980s when holding on to what has been achieved appears to be the order of the day. In its political substance *détente* is the necessary expression of the reality of Europe. It is thus a specifically European interest that the United States may not share as a primary concern but that becomes an Alliance interest if it is pursued in a sensible manner. Europe cannot accept total division. When the notion that strength will dissolve the other side and create unity on Western terms finally collapsed—which it did in the 1960s if it was ever seriously believed—the only option that remained open was to try to develop areas of common interest that did not touch on the sensitive core of different systems. The Helsinki process has become critical in this respect, although it is only a framework within which a hundred flowers of European cooperation can bloom. There is no need to repeat what was discussed earlier; but it may be worth adding a point of emphasis. If the United States should ever decide that the process of *détente* is undesirable and must be stopped, the effect on the Alliance would be serious. Europe would then be faced with the unacceptable choice between becoming a mere American satellite or falling prey to Soviet ambitions without any adequate defense.

Fifth, one of the important tasks of the decade is to develop a new partnership between the United States and Europe. Enough has been said about "partnership" and its limits to make it unnecessary to return to semantics. Suffice it to say that the need to which this conclusion alludes is not as commonplace as it may sound. The suggestion is not that new institutions should be created, not even that there should be a deliberate working-out of a program for partnership. (It could do no harm if foreign policy elites continued to devote their energy to the subject, as they have done in recent years.[18]) The suggestion is that a new appreciation of objectives, realities and interests should be sought to guide policy. There are times when having an analysis, and above all a shared analysis, is as important as having a program of action. As far as the Alliance is concerned, this may be such a time.

This essay is an attempt to contribute to an analysis of this

---

[18]At this point, at least, I must apologize to those friends and colleagues whose work I have used but not quoted, including the authors of important papers and books on Europe and America.

kind. It is therefore appropriate that the need for a new partnership should complete the summary of its argument. During the period of reconstruction after the war the Atlantic partnership grew naturally, albeit as one that we have described as all-embracing and almost familial. This was the time of the Pax Americana, the world order guaranteed by a benevolent United States of America. It was also the time when economic, social and political trends quite naturally brought Europe and America closer together. The period of reform in the 1960s and 1970s undoubtedly changed the picture in the sense of emphasizing differences. In socio-economic terms, what we have called "1968" produced a specifically European syndrome that for some is a source of pride and for others one of gloom, but which is certainly different from the American tradition. Politically, and notably in international politics, this was the period in which those things that were perceived to be in one's own and proper interest came to the fore on both sides of the Atlantic, and often at the expense of the institutions that were part-and-parcel of the postwar order. (Vietnam may well have been a mere accelerator of a process that was taking place in any case.) At first this process seemed to leave the Alliance unaffected, but as it went on it produced a number of irritants and a declining ability to understand the other.

The period of reversing trends (if that is what it is) in the 1980s has not yet led to any major improvement in Alliance relations. Yet the direction in which such improvement can be found has been well defined in America. Its name is burden-sharing. There is a specific issue of burden-sharing in defense, and it is real. It is probably not as much a conflict over the percentages of gross national product spent on defense or their increase as about real contributions to security. But this is not to detract from the importance of the subject. More important in terms of European-American relations, however, is the notion of an overall balance in trans-Atlantic relations, and one that is a negotiated balance. A wider sharing of the burden of preserving liberty and prosperity has to include defense as well as money and trade as well as development. There is no shortage of contentious issues in each of these fields. Without doubt, Europeans and Americans will take different stands on some of these issues in the international organizations in which they are discussed and even in bilateral talks. But in the end, it is the sharing of the burden of peace, prosperity and liberty in this wider sense that must provide the basis of a new contract of partnership.

For neither the Europeanization of Europe nor the Americanization of America needs to be seen as a threat. They are in fact quite normal developments, and even desirable. However, in order to be turned to advantage, the sense of anxiety and defensiveness that can sometimes be detected in them must be removed. A more American America has to come to terms with its world role and also with the fact that the world is a more varied and multidimensional place than some find it easy to accept. A more European Europe must learn to have the courage of its convictions, including maintaining its specific combination of security and flexibility, and must also evolve a plausible way for linking the overriding values of liberty and human rights with the undoubted interest in a wider Europe. In other words, both sides of the Atlantic need confidence. Success at home would help. So would a new group of powerful advocates of partnership in the Alliance.

Theodore C. Sorensen

A Changing America

A peacetime alliance of democracies is ultimately dependent for its success and survival upon widespread public support in each of its member countries. The Atlantic Alliance—because it relies heavily on the indefinite and expensive deployment of American armed forces in Europe 40 years after the close of the last European war and on America's continuing willingness to expose itself to nuclear obliteration as a deterrent to a Soviet attack in Western Europe—is singularly dependent on the steadfast support and understanding of the American public.

For more than 40 years, longer than any previous period in contemporary history, peace has prevailed in Europe at least in part because the members of the Atlantic Alliance, despite their widely divergent views and interests, have stuck together. For more than 40 years—despite recurring strains of doubt, disagreement, resentment and impatience—the American people have not basically challenged the sacrifice and risk inherent in Alliance membership.

But between now and the year 2000, public support for the Alliance on both sides of the Atlantic will be tested as never before. The small group of diplomats, businessmen, lawyers and academicians who forged the instruments of postwar unity has largely passed from the scene in both the United States and Western Europe. A new generation is assuming leadership, a generation whose foreign policy views were shaped more by the lessons of Vietnam than by the aggressions of Hitler and Stalin. The very success of the Alliance in diminishing any threat of a Soviet attack on Western Europe may cause many of the West's newer and younger leaders to question its relevance in today's world. The men and women who will increasingly control Western parliaments, cabinets and political parties over the next 15 years have given comparatively little thought to why their fathers and grandfathers founded a network of Atlantic institutions.

Moreover, many of the original assumptions underlying those institutions no longer prevail. No longer do majorities in either the United States or Western Europe believe they face a "clear and present danger" of deliberate Soviet attack or that the abnormal division of Germany and Europe can be peacefully ended in their lifetime. No longer do they expect the political and economic integration of Western Europe to produce in this century an equal diplomatic and military partner for the United States. Free trade across the Atlantic is no longer a realistic goal, and "traditional" market allocations mean little as competition for foreign sales intensifies between European and American exporters.

Perceptions have changed as well as assumptions. Although the Alliance in recent years has successfully withstood public protests and demonstrations against the deployment in Europe of American intermediate-range nuclear missiles and patched over its differences regarding the Soviet gas pipeline to the West, those episodes served to highlight the increasing divergence in U.S.-European perspectives on East-West relations. Given their greater geographic distance from Eastern Europe, it is not surprising that Americans know less about its history and culture than West Europeans, have less interest in it as either an export market or an energy and raw material source, and feel less of a direct stake in economic cooperation and political coexistence with it.

Most Americans believe they are as devoted to world peace and to the control of nuclear arms as the West Europeans. But not having suffered in this century the devastation by arms of their own homeland, Americans may not have fully grasped the depth of European fears—i.e., that their continent will involuntarily but inescapably become once again a principal theater of battle, this time to be permanently desolated by a clash between nuclear giants. An optimistic people by nature, most Americans are also more hopeful than their West European counterparts that both teams of negotiators at the Geneva arms control talks intend something more than a public relations charade.

American and European perceptions outside of Europe are diverging as well. America's attention is increasingly centered on dangers to peace and freedom in such Third World areas as Central America and the Middle East. Although our own citizenry is sharply divided on these issues, many Americans resent what they regard as European resistance to this country's leadership on a global scale. But the interests of Europeans extend beyond their own continent, and their views may increasingly irritate those Americans who expect unquestioning allied support outside of Europe, particularly in areas such as Central America where no European stake is acknowledged. Forgetting that we once offered friendly "advice"—and sometimes interference—regarding European roles in situations like the Suez crisis or the decolonization process, some Americans warn of diminished U.S. support for NATO if our allies do not demonstrate unswerving loyalty to America's unilateral course of action in Central America.

In this era of new strains, old strains persist: American complaints that our allies have consistently failed to meet their obligations to assume a fair share of NATO defense burdens in terms of both manpower and money, and European complaints that the United States has consistently failed to meet its obligation to consult before acting on all major issues affecting Western security; American resentment of European preaching about our Third World difficulties, and European resentment of American preaching about their economic difficulties; American fears that European resistance to new weapons systems will produce new Soviet divide-and-conquer tactics, and European fears that American resistance to new arms control initiatives will produce new Soviet aggression.

To be sure, disagreement and disappointment have characterized the Alliance since its inception. But most inter-allied differences in the past were confined largely to government officials. Those differences were successfully weathered by a generation of leaders who, if not all "present at the creation," were acutely mindful of the dangers that first led to the Alliance, were determined upon its success, and were understanding of each other's domestic political pressures. Those founding fathers have departed.

Could the disarray characterizing the Alliance in recent years drift before the end of the century into mutual disillusionment and disintegration? If so, the consequences for the Western democracies would be tragic: economic quarrels across the Atlantic followed by political and diplomatic quarrels, a withdrawal of U.S. troops from West Germany and a withdrawal of West German troops from NATO's integrated command, a move toward unilateralism in America followed by (or following) a move toward neutralism in Western Europe, a weakening of both the strength and the credibility of the Western deterrent followed by a weakening of the Western will to resist, a disillusioned Western Europe forsaking its role as American ally for that of an independent broker between the superpowers. That way lies the beginning of war or the end of liberty.

These are not the exaggerated nightmares of the traditional handwringing Atlanticist. Ronald Reagan's spring 1985 European tour, designed to halt this drift but dampened by protests over his visit to a West German cemetery where Nazi war dead were buried, was a mixed success at best. The Voice of America, customarily heard only in those foreign markets where local media are less sophisticated, is considering the resumption of broadcasting to Western Europe after a hiatus of a quarter-century on grounds that younger West Europeans, unappreciative of America's past ties and support, are too vulnerable to pro-Soviet, anti-American or neutralist propaganda.

That suspicion may be exaggerated. But I have no doubt that many West Europeans, convinced that the selfish cynicism of "Dallas" and "Dynasty" depict the true American character, are prepared to believe the worst. They are confronted with diametrically opposite messages from various self-appointed American "spokesmen," read widely divergent reports on polls surveying the American public's attitude toward its allies, and listen to American intellectuals of the left and right publicly attack each other's and the American government's credibility and courage in this openly self-critical society. It would hardly be surprising if some West Europeans felt tempted to declare a plague upon the houses of both superpowers, or to reject American leadership of the Alliance. Europe is changing, and its attitudes and responses can no longer be taken for granted.

But America, and its people, leadership and views, are also changing. It is not unnatural for West European opinion-makers, recognizing the value and frailty of the American relationship and comfortable with its original basis, to be fearful of change; and some of these evolutions in American perceptions and perspectives, as discussed below, do deserve particular European attention. But it is imperative that the real changes be distinguished from those that are merely alleged, the significant from the insignificant, the enduring from the ephemeral. It is imperative that Americans and West Europeans try to clear away the myths, clichés and stereotypes that too often clutter their trans-Atlantic debates and become more sensitive to each other's current thinking about the Alliance. That is the objective of this book.

I. Unfounded European Fears

Recent books, essays and speeches by a wide range of American pundits and politicians have sent differing signals to European eyes and ears, predicting *inter alia* the early demise of NATO, the erosion of Western Europe's importance to the United States, the withdrawal of one-half of American troops from Europe, and a refusal by the United States to undertake nuclear retaliation if ever needed in response to an overwhelming Soviet invasion of Europe. They have proposed an independent European defense force, a new Alliance Directorate, a "redefinition" of America's role in NATO, and even a termination of the Alliance. One slender volume on U.S.-European attitudes such as this, one unofficial American voice such as mine, cannot offset this cacophonous collection of American volumes and voices.

But a start can be made by addressing the five most common West European fears about American foreign policy, all of which I believe to be exaggerated. They are:

1) the fear that a militant right-wing unilateralism will drive America toward a nuclear holocaust;

2) the fear that a timid left-wing isolationism will cause America to abandon Europe at some future moment of peril;

3) the fear that the new economic power of the Pacific Basin will replace Western Europe in American affection, priorities and commitment;

4) the fear that America will disdain involvement with Western Europe as an economic "loser"; and

5) the fear that America will withdraw its troops from Europe to punish its allies for not doing more.

If these unfounded fears can be prevented or at least reduced, and no West European action is based upon them, then relations across the Atlantic will surely be stronger for the remainder of this century.

Let us examine each of these five fears.

Militant Right-Wing Unilateralism?

Most West European leaders have by now come to like Ronald Reagan as a genial politician whose Administration has helped restore American confidence and economic momentum. But his foreign policy rhetoric in the presidential campaign of 1980, followed by an overwhelming electoral victory and some bellicose talk by many of his appointees, sounded to many Europeans as though the United States had for the first time in the post-World War II era abandoned the path of collective restraint in East-West relations and embarked on a new solo course of assertive confrontation. Presidential references to the Soviet Union as the "focus of evil," to communism as a "bizarre chapter" in history whose last pages are "now being written," and loose Administration references to fighting and winning a nuclear war conjured up visions of an ideological messianic crusade against international communism, relying chiefly on the user or threat of force, with Western Europe serving as a helpless pawn and launching pad.

These fears have not been wholly allayed. Although the President's speeches, commencing with those delivered roughly one year before the 1984 elections, have sounded less belligerent toward the Soviet Union, they have still tended to view all world problems—including the Middle East, Central America, terrorism, and human rights—in East-West, good-versus-evil terms. Though altered in tone even more in the months preceding and following the Reagan-Gorbachev summit talk, they still often focused on halting the threat of aggression by the Soviet Union and its allies.

Though accustomed by now to both surprise and disappointment in American politics, West Europeans are not likely to look for leadership to a United States bent on exporting by direct or coercive action its political and economic system and values. Nor will they join in a new aggressive strategy for NATO seeking military supremacy over Moscow. In this context, they find particularly worrisome an apparently increased American willingness to act alone without awaiting or even seeking a NATO consensus. U.S. forces invaded Grenada, a member of the British Commonwealth, without consulting the British government. U.S. intelligence agents arranged to mine the harbors of Nicaragua without regard to allied ships plying those harbors. U.S. trade and defense officials pressured European subsidiaries and licensees of U.S. companies to halt their exports of technology to the Soviet Union without regard to the laws and policies of their host countries. U.S. rejection of a new Law of the Sea Treaty, and even the Administration's rejection of World Court jurisdiction in its dispute with Nicaragua, were regarded by some European critics as further evidence of a new U.S. unilateralism, a tendency to disregard both international friends and international principles whenever it deemed its own national interest to be at stake.

These anxieties were not confined to the West European peace movement, which some Administration officials dismissed as either cowardly or communist-inspired. Many European government officials, academics and editors—not all of them socialists, much less neutralists, pacifists or "unreliable wimps," as at least one anonymous Administration official charged—are fearful that the President neither means nor understands his new and softer line toward the Soviet Union and will not offer the genuine compromises necessary to reach an agreement at the Geneva arms reduction talks. One European leader, reviving the trigger-happy cowboy image that the Reagan reelection campaign has striven to erase, referred with colorful exaggeration last December to an "increasingly aggressive and ideological" American government that carried "a Bible in one hand and a revolver in the other."[1]

Much of this criticism was aimed at the Reagan Administration's policies in Central America, where the views of our Latin American friends were only perfunctorily sought and those of our European allies barely acknowledged. This display of unilateralism appeared less virulent in the direct East-West issues most affecting Europe. But then came President Reagan's surprise announcement of the Strategic Defense Initiative (SDI), and his subsequent insistence that it was nonnegotiable. Dismissing as futile and immoral (much as European pacifists have argued) the longstanding NATO doctrine of deterrence resting upon "mutual assured destruction"—long before any new doctrine (or the means to implement it) was ready as a replacement—the President publicly launched this significant change in the position of the West without any advance consultation with his allies. British and French discomfort may have been due at least in part to SDI's emasculatory effect, if implemented, on their independent nuclear arsenals. But many other Europeans fear an America relying on its own resources for its own defense, reducing its concern with the fate of Europe, eroding the 1972 Anti-Ballistic Missile Treaty that Europe had welcomed, and undermining any incentive for nuclear arms control while spurring a new arms race in space. Even if achievable, a world in which nuclear forces become obsolete might only be a world in which their continent was once again prey to devastation by conventional armies. Economic concern about further U.S. technological advantages over Western Europe as a consequence of SDI was also a factor in generating European concerns.

These may be premature reactions to a defensive system that is only in its earliest research stages (in both the U.S.S.R. and the United States)—particularly one that the Administration insists

---

[1]Paul Lewis, "It's Far from Quiet on the European Front," *The New York Times*, December 30, 1984, sec. 4, p. 4

helped spur greater Soviet interest in arms negotiations. Nevertheless, despite U.S. assurances and offers of technical cooperation, many Europeans, continued to view the Reagan SDI announcement as confirmation of the new American unilateralism.

Is unilateralism the path on which the United States is now permanently fixed? Should Europeans now believe that the American people have embraced what one British writer called "the language of domination and submission—the 'Dynasty' school of international relations?" Following the 1984 presidential election, many analysts concluded that a permanent realignment in American politics had occurred. A decisive long-term shift to the right, it was said, had resulted from an increase in southern and western electoral votes, an overwhelmingly prosperous electorate, a better organized and better financed Republican Party, an increase in the numbers and politicization of adherents to religious fundamentalism, and a more nationalistic, militaristic mood in the country. Only the aberrational post-Watergate, anti-Washington election of Jimmy Carter had interrupted this unstoppable trend, according to this view, which greatly troubled those Europeans hoping for a less confrontational world.

A more careful reading of the election data, however, indicates that Ronald Reagan's overwhelming victories in both 1980 and 1984 were more attributable to personal leadership and pocketbook issues than a mandate for international belligerence. Public frustration in 1980 over this country's inability to obtain the release of American diplomatic hostages in Iran or to prevent the Soviet invasion of Afghanistan helped President Carter's opponents portray him as ineffective; but foreign policy issues rarely determine American presidential elections (although they can influence each party's selection of a candidate), and 1980 was no exception. Both candidates condemned Soviet aggression and vowed to increase national defense, just as in 1984 both candidates pledged to meet with the Soviet leader and to negotiate arms limitations. In both elections, voters in both parties were far more interested in their respective presidential candidates' views on Social Security than national security. They voted for Ronald Reagan's telegenic warmth and confidence, and credited him in 1984 with the country's economic gains, even while disliking his foreign policy rhetoric. In 1984, the White House and the House of Representatives were won by opposite parties, each by a substantial margin. More voters still identify themselves as Democrats than as members of any other political party.

It is thus too early to conclude that a "sea change" has occurred in American politics, bringing a long-term realignment on the right comparable to the 1932 shift to the left. There is reason for hope—although less in the short run, to be sure—that in time the American people will exercise their new-found power in foreign affairs (described below) to turn this country back from the path of aggressive unilateralism. Indeed, in 1985 both President Reagan and Secretary of State George Shultz came under increasing fire from the far right for practicing restraint in international affairs, seeking increased dialogue with Moscow, and accepting equivalence in strategic power. Nicaragua has not been invaded; NATO has not been abandoned; no attempt has been made to liberate Eastern Europe or, in a serious way, Afghanistan.

Americans may be more accustomed than their European cousins to a gap between presidential oratory and conduct. Some of the tough talk, we realize, is meant only for a selected domestic audience to shore up political support on the right. Some of it is designed to rally public backing for ever greater military budgets. It does not signify, at least on the crucial issues, a permanent substitution of right-wing unilateralism for our customarily pragmatic internationalism. True, most Americans remain more mistrustful than Europeans are of the Soviet Union, more likely to regard it as a constant military threat, more assertive in their idealistic support of the human rights denied by Moscow, and more confident that the future will prove us right and the Kremlin wrong. But even a president further to the right in international affairs than Reagan (unlikely) would find it difficult, if not impossible, to impose an anti-Soviet military crusade on an American Congress and public that have made clear their dislike for confrontational tactics, their deep opposition to the use of nuclear weapons, and their devout wish for an end to the arms race and worldwide tensions.

Timid Left-Wing Isolationism?

During the 1961 Berlin crisis, when Soviet Chairman Nikita S. Khrushchev warned President John F. Kennedy that a new treaty would soon extinguish the Western allies' right of access to West Berlin, two fears prevailed in much of Western Europe: fear that the Americans would not stand firm and fear that they would. This same "nuclear schizophrenia" has often characterized Europe's concern about the American finger on the nuclear trigger. If, in response to a threatened or actual Soviet invasion of Europe, a "macho" America insisted on quickly pulling that trigger, all of Europe could be lost; but if a weak-willed America shrank from pulling that trigger, all of Europe could be lost. Moreover, if that weakness of will were deduced in advance by Moscow and the world, West Europeans could no longer look to the Atlantic Alliance for their security, and a spate of individual deals and independent nuclear deterrents would soon produce a less stable world.

In that context, the strength of the anti-nuclear movement in the United States—initially welcomed by many Europeans as a curb on the new militance of the right—would give them concern if it appeared to be pushing a substantial segment of the American electorate and Congress toward a new isolationism on the left. Conservative U.S. commentators and politicians have increasingly accused post-Vietnam liberals of weakening the nation's readiness and resolve to intervene militarily whenever and wherever our interest so requires. These "doves," they charge, who "blame America first" and hesitate to use force against poorly armed Marxists in America's "own backyard," will never summon the courage to stand up in Europe to a Soviet juggernaut that these "misguided leftists" view as the "moral equivalent of American imperialism." Listening to all this, many Europeans, who feel that their ultimate security depends upon the credibility of the American nuclear guarantee—i.e., upon a Russian conviction that we Americans will risk our lives and cities if the lives and cities of Western Europe are threatened— may well find deeply disturbing the prospect that a future Congress or White House controlled by liberals would renounce any first use of nuclear weapons even against a Soviet conventional military force overrunning Western Europe.

The worst kind of crisis that can confront the Western Alliance is a crisis of confidence—including a lack of European confidence in either America's reliability as an ally, or America's willingness to respond with nuclear weapons when necessary. The need for that confidence lies at the very heart of the Alliance's political design and military planning. Any unfounded charges in this country that undermine that confidence and create in Europe a fear of being left alone do a grave disservice to Western security.

Would such a fear be unfounded? To be sure, a recurrent strain of isolationism, a traditional rejection of foreign entanglements, has never been very far beneath the surface of the American polity. This was true even after World War II and the development of intercontinental ballistic missiles had made clear that our ocean surroundings no longer offered meaningful protection in a dangerous world. At times isolationism crops up on the right with denouncements of the United Nations, foreign economic assistance, Third World socialists, and ungrateful Western allies who do not support our every action. At other times it crops up on the left with denouncements of all military pacts and arms sales, and opposition to the dispatch of U.S. military advisers, assistance or forces to any foreign battle. At still other times, including the period just prior to the Second World War, it attracts converts from both left and right in both major parties.

In recent public opinion polls,[2] the American people (especially Democrats, liberals, moderates, young people, minorities and women—though all political and demographic lines are

---

[2]It is not possible to list here all the polls consulted and their sponsors and dates of publication. The bulk was provided by Potomac Associates, Washington, D.C., William Watts, President, with field work conducted by the Gallup Organization. Another principal source was a series of surveys conducted in 1975, 1978, and 1982 by the Chicago Council on Foreign Relations, edited by John E. Reilly, President. A principal source was "Voter Options on Nuclear Arms Policy," published in 1984 by the Public Agenda Foundation of New York, Daniel Yankelovich, President.

crossed) have appeared to be more preoccupied with their domestic economic concerns and thus less interested in military or even diplomatic cooperation with our allies and less willing to deploy more American forces in response to Soviet aggression in peripheral areas. In sharp contrast with 1980, when a series of disturbing developments in Iran, Afghanistan, Poland and Cuba aroused the public's anger, Americans today are less enthusiastic about a larger and more expensive U.S. military establishment. Above all, they are increasingly anxious about the possibility of nuclear war and global annihilation. (Most Americans mistakenly assume that "no-first-use" of nuclear weapons, even against Soviet conventional forces overrunning U.S. and allied forces in Western Europe, is our policy now—and they approve of that policy.)

Because these rank-and-file views frequently find expression in the platforms, speeches and articles of various political candidates, their opponents often charge them with preaching isolationism. A perusal of the 1984 national convention platforms of both parties, however, finds both of them condemning Soviet aggression, emphasizing the importance and indivisibility of the Atlantic Alliance, supporting a strong defense, avoiding any call for American troop withdrawals from Europe, stressing the need for a balance of conventional forces, and invoking the examples of earlier presidents who used force selectively to protect U.S. interests while preferring peaceful over military solutions.

But do the aforementioned public opinion surveys indicate a trend toward isolationism in the general public? Poll results must be read and interpreted with care. American public opinion on foreign policy can be volatile, arbitrary, sometimes poorly informed or hastily conceived. Different wording of the same question can produce different results. Answers to hypothetical questions can change dramatically in a short period if the hypothesis becomes a reality. The public mood of the moment on a particular issue is often sharply different from the ultimate public judgment on that issue formulated over a period of time primarily by those who have examined it seriously.

Some questions to the general public—such as the quality of allied relations, or an assignment of blame for poor allied relations, or the consequences of a communist party electoral victory in an allied state—produce answers of little real value to decision-makers. Yes or no answers to necessarily simplified questions may not reveal the extent to which the respondent knows about the issue, cares about the issue, or is influenced by the issue in casting his vote. This is particularly true regarding questions on foreign affairs in general and Alliance commitments in particular; for, most people in this country have no sustained interest or involvement in foreign affairs and no strong opinions on Alliance commitments. Moreover, a substantial number of those polled do not vote; and, as already noted, those who do vote rarely make up their minds on the basis of foreign policy issues.

Nevertheless, careful comparisons of limited polling data over a period of time can be useful, not to dictate a congressman's vote or a president's action (which would be contrary to the concept of a representative system) but to indicate possible long-term directions in public thinking as distinguished from temporary detours. Marginal changes are not meaningful. Even substantial changes on issues beyond public understanding or likely public influence can be discounted. But successful presidents and congressional leaders reach their high stations by sensing and reflecting, as well as influencing, long-term trends in public opinion; and comparative poll data can thus often indicate policy developments as well as current attitudes.

In undertaking this assignment I have reviewed the results of hundreds of polls taken over the last four decades. My own analysis, although confirming some potential weakness in future Alliance support as indicated above, concludes that, on balance, it is grossly inaccurate to label the American majority with an isolationist tag.

Some in-depth surveys in foreign policy, particularly those conducted over the years for the Chicago Council on Foreign Relations, undertake to divide (or their results can be used to divide) public responses under four overlapping labels:

• *internationalism*, championing a prominent U.S. role in the world through military, economic and diplomatic cooperation with our allies and others;

• *interventionism*, favoring direct U.S. action in world trouble spots, usually by the threat or use of armed force or dispatch of military assistance;

• *unilateralism*, preferring a "go-it-alone" course of intervention regardless of allied views; and

• *isolationism*, placing a higher priority on this country's domestic needs and questioning any U.S. obligation to protect other nations against internal or external threats.

Such distinctions are necessarily rough and arbitrary, but their use is nevertheless illuminating over a long period. This analysis confirms what many political leaders have already sensed—that a steady decline in public internationalism and interventionism occurred during the disillusioning years when U.S. forces were fighting in Vietnam; that isolationism during that period rose, but not proportionately and—like unilateralism—has never reflected a majority view; and that, since the mid-1970s, internationalism has regained strength, and both isolationism and unilateralism have declined. Interventionism, which also regained strength as the grip of Vietnam on the public psyche faded, reached a peak in 1980—a year of public anger, as previously mentioned—but otherwise never matched the rise of internationalism.

Surprisingly, no meaningful differences on these internationalist-isolationist scales appear between Republicans and Democrats. Internationalist attitudes do rise steadily with levels of formal education as well as income, an encouraging sign in a country with an increasingly high proportion of high school and college graduates.

Interventionism's lag behind internationalism indicates that selectivity, rather than isolationism (or neutralism or pacifism), now governs American attitudes toward the use of force, as discussed further below. Different polls at different times using different wording have in recent years produced widely different answers regarding the use of U.S. troops to defend Western Europe in the event of a Soviet invasion. Nevertheless, all but one of the latest polls on this subject have consistently shown greater support than outright opposition to such a position, greater support than was true a decade ago, and greater support for defending Western Europe under direct attack than any other current danger spot in the world. (The use of U.S. troops if Middle East oil supplies to Western Europe were cut off, for example, was not supported.) On this issue, liberals, conservatives, Democrats and Republicans—although dividing along predictable lines regarding military spending—produced roughly the same proportion of affirmative answers.

Indeed, NATO and the members of the Atlantic Alliance generally have enjoyed a majority of support along the American political and ideological spectrum, rising over the last decade with other manifestations of internationalism, but never falling into serious disfavor even during the Vietnam War years of disenchantment. American opinion polls did not even support the Reagan sanctions on European contracts for the Soviet gas pipeline.

True, questions on nuclear weapons elicit a different kind of reaction. Most Americans, left and right, state now that they do not want to see U.S. nuclear weapons used even in response to Soviet tanks conquering Europe. But West European leaders, whose own public opinion polls have shown an equally strong opposition to the use of nuclear weapons and even less support for the Atlantic Alliance, need not fear that this portends a U.S. move toward isolationism. To be sure, the American people are not belligerent and eager to do battle, especially nuclear battle; but the same polls show that they do support a posture of nuclear retaliation for a Soviet first-strike and do prefer the risk of death and devastation at home to imposition of the Soviet system. Whatever doubts they may have had after Vietnam about playing a role on the international stage, any president whose prudence and discretion they trust will have majority support in whatever measured actions he feels obligated to take in meeting this country's most important international commitments. That qualified conclusion will not reassure those Europeans who seek some kind of unlimited and irreversible pledge; but few if any unlimited and irreversible pledges about anything remain in American foreign policy.

A Pacific Basin Priority?

One significant change in America's international posture in the last decade is undeniable. The nations of the Pacific Basin—Japan, China and others—now exercise a growing political and economic impact on this country that is receiving increased attention from our executive and legislative branches of government, our colleges and universities, our news and entertainment media, our business leaders and the general public. Simultaneously, political and economic power in this country has appeared to shift from the industrial states on the Atlantic seaboard (traditionally the strongest supporters of the Alliance) to the "Sunbelt" states of the Southwest (more Latin America-oriented in their outlook) and West (more Pacific-oriented). In addition, as the result of sweeping changes in U.S. immigration patterns over the last 20 years, new citizens from Asia—more than half of whom live in California—greatly outnumber new immigrants from Europe, and the Asian population in this country is expected to double by the year 2010. (Although the increase in the size and voting power of Latin American immigrants and their children in this country is far greater, European fears of being displaced seem to center on the Pacific.)

Will these changes reduce American support for the Alliance? NATO was approved by the U.S. Senate in 1949 over the protests of conservative Republicans and "China Lobby" spokesmen who urged an "Asia first" policy. Now both parties in their national platforms have taken to terming the United States "a Pacific power" (although the Democratic platforms, except during the Vietnam War, have consistently devoted more attention to Western Europe than to Asia). From the days of General Douglas MacArthur, who predicted that America's true destiny would be fulfilled in the Pacific, to the observation in March 1984 of then-Under Secretary of State Lawrence Eagleburger of a continuing westward shift in our political center of gravity, American leaders have spoken increasingly about the importance to this country of the Pacific Basin. There, said U.S. Ambassador to Japan Mike Mansfield, citing the statements of President Reagan and Secretary of State Schultz, is "where it all is, what it is all about, and where our future lies."[3]

Even applying the customary discount required for diplomatic overstatement, West European leaders watching this apparent trend might well speculate on their future standing in America's order of priority. The Norwegian Ambassador to the United Nations, Tom Eric Vraalsen, noting these demographic changes, concluded that the United States was bound to pay more attention to its Pacific Basin relations. From less time and attention to less importance and affection to less concern and commitment are not large steps.

But Americans are not taking those steps; and statistics whether demographic or economic, can be misleading, if not irrelevant. A half-century ago, when this nation was overwhelmingly of European stock, we were not pro-Europe but isolationist, often anti-Europe, against the "Old World." It is true that the number of new entrants into this country from Europe, once virtually the sole source of all U.S. immigration, now trails far behind the total of those entering from Latin America and Asia; that the proportion of Americans of non-European origin has more than doubled since the founding of the Alliance; and that Asian-Americans—who now comprise some 40 percent of all newcomers to the United States—have more than doubled their proportion in the U.S. population. But that proportion is still less than 2 percent, and Asian-American leaders and voters have shown no interest in weakening our commitment to NATO. Similarly, although it is true that the number of U.S. college students studying French and German has sharply declined, that is part of an unfortunate decline in nearly all foreign language studies (other than Spanish), not remotely offset by an increase in the tiny proportion of those learning Japanese and Chinese.

It is also true that American trade with the countries of the Pacific Basin has surpassed our trade with Western Europe, that Asia is the fastest growing market for U.S. manufactured exports and the largest supplier of U.S. imports, and that the

---

[3]Speech at the Annual Japan Society Dinner, New York, N.Y., March 19, 1985; see also *The Nihon Keizai Shimbun (Japan Economic Journal)*, May 1, 1984, p. 24.

economic and technological development of Japan in particular has riveted the political as well as commercial attention of this country. But Western Europe continues to be of the utmost economic importance to the United States. To date, the level of U.S. investment in Europe, and the level of European investment in the United States, substantially exceed their U.S.-Pacific counterparts. The same is true of travel by European tourists in America, and American tourists in Europe, compared to their statistical Pacific-U.S. counterparts. Western Europe is still the largest concentration of economic power in the world, with a gross national product (GNP) and standard of living well above those of the Pacific Basin. (Moreover, with protectionist tempers rising, Japan's increasing role as an exporter of manufactured goods to this country has incurred U.S. public and political resentment far beyond that stirred by America's trade problems with Europe.)

It is true, finally, that the New England and Mid-Atlantic states now have a smaller proportion of population—and thus fewer congressional seats and presidential electors—than they had when NATO was first approved (New York and Pennsylvania alone, for example, have lost more than 20 congressional seats through reapportionment); true that the political as well as economic power of the Pacific Coast and other western states has sharply increased, as that region's share of U.S. population overtakes the Northeast (although migration from the Northeast to the Sunbelt has recently ended as the former's economy substantially revived and the energy-rich economy of the latter declined); and true that the Pacific states have traditionally and not surprisingly been more eager than any other section of the country to look across the Pacific for political as well as commercial ties. But western Americans and their representatives in Congress have proven to be no less committed to the Atlantic Alliance than are those who reside on the Atlantic Coast or elsewhere.

In poll after poll over the years, Americans have repeatedly been asked which group of friendly nations is more important to the United States, those of Asia or those of Western Europe; and whether the United States should help out militarily if Western Europe, or Japan, or Korea came under attack. In virtually every case, the commitment to Western Europe was substantially higher, and that margin has increased over the years even as U.S.-Pacific economic ties and the non-European component of our population became stronger.

America's ties with Europe are based on more than economics, demographics and geography. We are bound together in a community of values and interests, by a common political and cultural heritage and history. Those bonds are not displaced, nor their strength diminished, by the Pacific Basin's rise in importance and economic strength. Europeans must understand that their continent does not enjoy the same monopoly on American time, energy and attention that it once enjoyed, and that this trend will continue, particularly as Asia looms larger economically and this country's Hispanic population increases. American diplomacy should be sensitive to their concern on this point, making clear that this is not a matter of "either-or." But the United States could not accept a world in which Western Europe was controlled by hostile forces. That is why, except for one brief period during the Vietnam War, the bulk of America's overseas forces has been stationed in Western Europe, not in Asia or the Pacific Basin. Europe remains and will long remain among our highest priorities.

A Disdained Economic "Loser"?

"The Americans like to deal only with successful people, not with losers," said a leading French economist, Michel Albert, recently with reference to all of Western Europe, "and there is no question that we're the losers right now."[4] This reflection of "Europessimism" is rooted primarily in the disparity between Europe's economic growth and America's. That is not the exclusive cause—many Europeans are reportedly dissatisfied as well with the slow pace of their political integration, their reduced importance in the councils of world power, and their diminished role in new technological and intellectual developments. They

---

[4]Scott Sullivan, "The Decline of Europe," *Newsweek*, April 9, 1984, p. 44.

see America becoming more innovative and dynamic, its citizens filled with more pride, confidence and motivation.

But nearly all of these feelings are related to America's resumption of noninflationary economic growth and productivity in recent years while Europe's economy—at least until recently—has stood still by comparison. Over the last decade, 15 million to 18 million new jobs were created in the United States while 1.5 million to 2 million jobs were lost in Europe. A U.S. unemployment level of seven percent, now largely, if reluctantly, accepted as "normal," is well above our old national goal of four percent but well below the figures now prevailing in most of Europe, including those countries that once enjoyed consistently lower unemployment than the United States. (Ironically, what little economic growth that did occur recently in several of Europe's leading industrialized states was due in substantial part to purchases by American importers and tourists.) Meanwhile, as previously mentioned, American businessmen have paid increasing attention to Pacific markets and trading partners.

Does this stamp Europe as a "loser" unworthy of American support? References to "Eurosclerosis" in the U.S. press and economic literature have been frequent, invariably followed by patronizing diagnoses of Europe's labor-market rigidities, excessive welfare and tax burdens, nationalized industries, disincentives to innovation, and other structural causes of economic malaise. Europe's much higher level of payroll and social security costs, much higher proportion of workers covered by collective bargaining contracts, and much higher degree of government ownership and intervention in the market, have made it less responsive than America (and Japan), the critics say, to today's entrepreneurial and technological revolutions that are substituting new "high tech" and service (i.e., financial, retail, information, telecommunication, health and other) jobs for the declining "smokestack" industry jobs more cheaply performed in less developed countries or by robots.

Europeans, unwilling to place full blame for their sluggish economic performance on their traditional preference for job stability, point to the loss of European investment funds attracted to the United States not only by the size, strength and security of the U.S. market but also by the high interest rates, substantial credit requirements and overvalued dollar created by America's enormous budget deficits. They also note that Europe's economic growth and anti-inflation efforts, unlike America's, do not depend on vast budget and trade deficits and foreign capital inflow. They acknowledge that their political traditions and pressures do not enable them to match America in economic deregulation, but they are nevertheless making some moves in that direction, encouraging private initiative, curbing inflation, restoring profits and increasing investment—all while resisting deficit spending more effectively than has the United States, where economic growth appeared to pause in the summer of 1985.

"Winners" and "losers" in national economics are never permanent. (Not so long ago Americans were marvelling at the West German economic "miracle.") Neither the United States nor Western Europe has produced an acceptable long-term answer to today's economic problems. Neither can be certain of the duration of its present economic condition. The technological internationalization of the market place has increased the value, velocity and volatility of economic transactions and problems beyond the manageability of any single nation or geographic grouping of nations. The growing gap between rich and poor nations—like the gap between rich and poor in our own nation—cannot long continue without an explosion engulfing us all.

Any feelings of U.S. superiority or European resentment on economic grounds can only hinder the cooperation that is essential not only to advance our mutual security but also to halt the tide of protectionism now rising on both sides of the Atlantic. This could pose a threat to the Alliance greater than any mentioned above. Protectionism, whether it comes in the name of "sectoral reciprocity," "voluntary" quotas, "industrial policy" or some other new label, could divide the Alliance more quickly than European neutralism, more effectively than Soviet propaganda, more decisively than U.S. unilateralism.

Unfortunately more protectionist proposals have been introduced in the U.S. Congress over the last 4 years than in the previous 40 combined. The traditional pro-trade stance of the House of Representatives Democratic majority has eroded sharply, reflecting public opinion polls showing that even farmers and consumers now support limitations on imports. Thus far Japan—and to a lesser extent Korea, Hong Kong and other East Asian jurisdictions—have been the prime target of official wrath. But there is growing resentment with regard to European trade barriers to U.S. exports (in agriculture and telecommunications, for example) and cheap European exports (such as steel) to the United States.

An all-out trade war across the Atlantic would seriously weaken allied unity and security. So would a U.S.-European Economic Community failure to reach agreement on the extent to which their respective markets should be open to East Asian and Third World exports. So would a massive electoral repudiation of those European governments most supportive of the Alliance by voters dissatisfied with continuing high unemployment. So would a continuing long-term decline in Western Europe's economic capacity to afford its share of the NATO deterrent, or to participate in high technology that increasingly underlies it. In short, Americans are the ultimate losers when Europe lags economically. Increasingly aware of our own unacceptably high trade and budget deficits and the recent signs of weakness in our own economic growth, we are in no position to dismiss Europeans as "losers." Very few do.

U.S. Troop Withdrawal?

No issue has caused more persistent and painful disputes between the United States and Western Europe over the last two decades than the question of Alliance "burden-sharing" in general and the level of European-based U.S. troops in particular.

Although both the number and percentage of U.S. military personnel stationed overseas have fluctuated since the end of the Second World War, ranging between two-tenths and three-tenths of the total, depending upon world conditions, the largest proportion of those forces both before and after the Vietnam War has been based in Europe. Most of them—the equivalent of five Army divisions (with pre-positioned equipment for three to four more)—are near the border between East and West Germany.

The United States, despite its rising budget deficits, has been consistently devoting to military spending a much higher proportion of its GNP and overall government budget than have its European allies. The agreed-upon NATO target in 1978 of an annual three-percent-above-inflation increase for five years in each member's defense spending was only the latest such commitment to be fulfilled by the United States but virtually ignored by our principal European allies—some of whom even reduced their defense budgets. Not surprisingly, a series of warnings, complaints and threats to withdraw U.S. troops has emanated every year for 20 years from frustrated American legislators and foreign policy commentators.

West European officials regard the level of U.S. forces on their continent as a barometer of our commitment. Yet the indefinite presence of foreign troops in any free and peaceful country requires an explanation. Even Dwight Eisenhower originally intended only a temporary deployment of U.S. forces in Europe until that continent could organize its own defense. In recent months, a number of respected U.S. experts have urged a reduction or withdrawal of U.S. forces from Europe, arguing variously that U.S. "solvency and safety" require it, or that a larger European responsibility for self-defense would accelerate European unity, or that U.S. commitments elsewhere in the world require a redeployment from Europe. Two-thirds of all Americans surveyed in a 1983 poll felt that the United States was shouldering too much of the Western security burden and that Western Europe was shouldering too little.

The issue is closely related to the deep unease on both continents over the use of nuclear weapons. If Warsaw Pact ground forces were ever to overrun NATO ground forces, according to NATO doctrine, NATO would respond with nuclear weapons. Some have long argued that the symbolic (and far more economical) presence of one "tripwire" or "plate glass" platoon would make it far clearer to the Soviets that any invasion would immediately incur "massive retaliation." But for well over a decade U.S. and NATO leaders have preferred a wider range of options than nuclear war or surrender in the event of a Soviet attack, as well as more time to prevent a nuclear exchange and to decide on their choice of options.

According to this prevailing view, the greater NATO's comparative strength is on the ground, the less likely it is that nuclear war will have to be unleashed in response to a Soviet incursion. Conversely, the more NATO fails to build conventional strength, the more likely is the prospect of someday facing an unappetizing choice between a Soviet military conquest of Western Europe or Western resort to the tactical, intermediate-range and strategic nuclear weapons that will place American as well as European populations at risk. Seen in that light, a NATO force lacking the ability to resist conventional attack would soon lack the necessary confidence of parliaments and citizens on both sides of the Atlantic.

In a logical world, Europeans could be certain that the United States, no matter how often it complained that their insufficient efforts were lowering the nuclear threshold, would never in retaliation proceed to lower that threshold still further by withdrawing U.S. ground forces from the continent. But logic does not always prevail even between the most intelligent and civilized of nations. Angered by Western Europe's consistent inability to meet its share of NATO spending and personnel targets, irritated by disputes with Europe over trade and Central America, indignant that Europe would complain under these circumstances about *our* budget deficits, pressured at home by the dwindling but nevertheless noisy voices of unilateralism on the right and isolationism on the left, a solid bloc of U.S. senators and congressmen for two decades has regularly urged such a withdrawal.

First formally proposed by liberal Senate Democrat Mike Mansfield in 1966, and annually thereafter for eight years, the initial troop-withdrawal amendment took on a variety of forms, each calling for a substantial but not total reduction. It had important support—including that of the Chairman of the Senate Foreign Relations Committee, the Chairman of the Senate Armed Services Committee, the members of the Senate Democratic Policy Committee, and 44 co-sponsors from both parties. One year it was temporarily approved, then defeated. Another year 60 of the Senate's 100 members approved one or another of the many versions offered.

In 1974 the opposition to Mansfield was led by a conservative Democrat. Sam Nunn, one of the most knowledgeable members of the Armed Services Committee, a strong NATO supporter, and author of his own compromise requiring a gradual withdrawal of U.S. forces if our allies did not meet their fair share of NATO costs. That approach, in principle not unlike Mansfield's, was the forerunner of the 1984 Nunn Amendment, co-sponsored by both liberals and conservatives in both parties. That amendment would have withdrawn nearly one-third of the American troops in Western Europe by 1990 if our allies did not increase their contributions to the levels previously agreed upon. Senator Nunn has asked why the United States should spend more when its allies do not meet their commitments.

> We are spending enormous amounts of money on defense, particularly NATO defense, that has no significant military effect unless the allies do their part. We might as well be throwing the money away. . . . But you really have to question why you need 300,000 troops over there to be there for a few days before you start shooting nuclear weapons."[5]

His was not the only, or even the fiercest, voice in the nation advocating U.S. troop withdrawals. Cartoonist Bill Mauldin, liberal, internationalist, pro-Europe, depicted two Europeans saying to each other in the Café des Bruxelles: "We will defend ourselves to the last American." Conservative Republican Congressman John McCain, a war hero, former Navy Captain, and the son and grandson of admirals, has asked how large a U.S. presence in Europe is warranted given NATO's "parsimonious" attitude. Democratic Presidential candidate John Glenn warned: "Americans ultimately will find it unacceptable to pay a disproportionate share to do for Europe what the Europeans can be doing for themselves. . . ."[6] Secretary of Defense Weinberger

---

[5]Michael R. Gordon, "Nunn: More to Do," interview in *Military Logistics Forum*, March 1985, p. 28.

[6]"Rethinking Defense," in Glenn et al., *Rethinking Defense and Conventional Forces*, Washington, D.C.: Center for National Policy, 1983, Alternatives for the 1980's, no. 8, p. 12.

similarly predicted: "The American people may not wish to bear the burden of necessary defense expenditures if they think some are doing less as we do more."[7]

Nevertheless the Nunn Amendment lost. The Mansfield Amendment lost. Other than marginal reductions unrelated to NATO costs, all such amendments have always ultimately lost. No administration has ever supported a troop-withdrawal amendment, all prediction to the contrary notwithstanding. Conservatives warned Europe that a Democratic administration would carry out the Mansfield Amendment—but Carter did not. Liberals warned Europe that a Republican administration would withdraw into a Fortress America—but Reagan did not. On the contrary, the national platforms of the two major political parties, although urging increased European contributions to NATO, have never urged substantial troop withdrawal—with the single exception of the 1972 (McGovern) Democratic Convention platform. U.S. public opinion poll respondents, although complaining regularly about disproportionate burden-sharing, have in those same polls maintained their support for the Alliance and for the U.S. commitment to it; and public support for a troop-withdrawal amendment has steadily declined since "non-internationalist" sentiment peaked in the mid-1970s.

Moreover, this rejection of U.S. troop withdrawals as a means of protesting Europe's lagging efforts has been voiced without extensive awareness on the part of the American public of precisely what our allies are contributing to the collective defense of Europe—by their count 90 to 95 percent of the ground forces, 80 to 85 percent of the tanks, 80 percent of the combat aircraft and 70 percent of the fighting ships. No doubt some Europeans do prefer to let Uncle Sam carry the burden, or believe a lower nuclear threshold is a more convincing deterrent, or fear that increasing their conventional forces might provoke Moscow. But that is not the posture of the continent as a whole. Our European allies, some by use of a compulsory draft, pay for a million more men under arms than the United States, and give proportionately greater economic assistance to the developing worlds.

---

[7]Richard Halloran, "Arms for Jordan Will Be Pressed by Weinberger," *The New York Times*, February 14, 1982, sec. 1, p. 1.

Though handicapped by serious fiscal and economic problems in the 1980s, Western Europe's proportionate increases in defense spending generally exceeded those of the United States in the 1970s. No doubt the U.S.S.R. wishes that its allies made a contribution to Warsaw Pact preparedness comparable to that which our allies make to the NATO common defense.

It is a common defense. Western Europe is the forward defense line of the United States. Our forces are there not out of charity but self-interest. Their unilateral withdrawal would reduce the nuclear threshold, undo the political bargain that supports the military alliance, discourage further West European efforts, encourage Soviet intransigence in the Mutual and Balanced Force Reduction talks and other negotiations, reduce the strength and credibility of our deterrent and undermine our security. Withdrawing the troops while continuing both the cost of maintaining them here and the commitment to send them back when needed would save very few dollars at very great expense. The one cost we cannot afford is the cost of either allies or Soviets doubting whether American ground forces would be there at the required moment. No doubt our Congress, public opinion and emerging new opinion-makers need constant reminders of all this, as a Soviet ground attack in Europe seems increasingly unlikely. But that is what leadership is for, particularly presidential leadership.

Recent NATO improvements in munition stocks, reinforcement facilities, and otherwise have reduced the calls in Congress for troop withdrawals. But, for the reasons stated above, it is doubtful that the votes were ever there anyway. Future U.S. force reductions as the result of new strategy, technology or NATO planning should never be ruled out; but withdrawal as a method of punishing or pressuring Western Europe seems unlikely in this century, assuming no serious inter-allied dispute of the kind previously mentioned. The fear that the Congress will someday soon adopt, and the president sign and implement, one of the periodic reincarnations of Mansfield-Nunn is an unfounded fear, a fear which—like the other four fears discussed—should not be allowed to distort U.S.-West European relations.

II. The Changing American Scene

It should be clear from the foregoing that America today is vastly different from the America that first joined in the establishment of the Western Alliance, but that "every difference does not make a difference" and that those differences set forth above are not valid grounds for European fears. It is important to the future success of the Alliance that those fears be prevented or allayed and not acted upon. But some differences do make a difference; and it is equally important to the future success of the Alliance that Europe and the world recognize and adjust their thinking to three fundamental changes in the American scene over the last decade or more that could alter the way this country approaches international affairs. They are: (1) the democratization of American foreign policy decision-making; (2) the Vietnam War's impact on American foreign policy decision-making; and (3) the emergence of a new generation of American foreign policy decision-makers.

Democratization

Within the federal government, foreign policy decision-making was once largely the preserve of the president and his secretary of state. No longer. Outside the federal government, foreign policy influence—particularly on Alliance issues—was once largely the preserve of a small elite "establishment" and a handful of internationalist newspapers. No more.

For over two decades after the close of the Second World War, the power structure of American foreign policy was a steep pyramid. At the top was the president and just beneath him his secretaries of state and defense. Beneath them were a tiny handful of other key executive branch appointees, then a larger group from State and other departments, followed by key congressional leaders. Not far from the top was a small, largely homogeneous "establishment" elite of private opinion-leaders, lawyers, bankers and others, who moved in and out of government councils and official positions, as well as columnists and editorial writers for *The New York Times* and *The Washington Post*. The wider and deeper layers below were occupied by a larger number of congressmen, journalists and citizens who were knowledgeable about foreign affairs but whose influence was limited. At the bottom of the pyramid was the general public, empowered every four years to vote for a president but largely inattentive to and uninformed about most foreign policy issues except in times of crisis.

Over the last decade and a half, both power and information in that pyramid have seeped downward. The pyramid remains. The president still has ultimate authority. Members of the expert foreign policy establishment, now far more open, divided and broad-based, still have more influence than uninterested members of the general public. But the role and influence of each layer of that pyramid have been dramatically altered.

The reassertion by Congress of its constitutional role in the guidance of American foreign policy has been amply described elsewhere. Legislators in both Houses oversee foreign operations as well as policy, battlefield tactics as well as strategy, weapons specifications as well as quantities, and individual product quotas as well as trade laws. Bipartisanship in foreign policy is invoked by whichever party controls the executive branch but with very little effect. Total legislative deference to the president in foreign affairs, requiring of him neither compromise nor concession, is largely a phenomenon of the past. Although frequent references to the spectacle of 535 congressmen and senators each acting like a little secretary of state may be exaggerated, an estimated 75 separately motivated legislators today do exercise substantial influence over foreign policy decisions.

European ambassadors and visiting foreign officials in Washington find they must appeal to or even negotiate with Congress as well as the White House and State Department. Special interest groups, ethnic lobbyists and ideological organizations, often backed by political campaign contributions, have gained greater influence on issues of trade, military assistance and economic development. Congress sends its own observers to international negotiations. Individual members meet not only with heads of state but also with leaders of the political opposition and even rebel movements as well.

Moreover, just as foreign policy influence within the executive branch itself has become more broadly dispersed (with White House staff and a number of departments and agencies now playing more significant roles), so also has legislative responsibility in this area spread from the once all-powerful Senate Foreign Relations Committee to a dozen or more others. As the number of senators and congressmen with long seniority declined between 1971 and 1981 (the median years of service in the Senate dropped by more than 50 percent), and the number of first-term members increased (constituting over half the Senate in 1981), seniority counted for less. Newcomers found themselves chairing Senate subcommittees. An old-timer was ousted as chairman of the House Armed Services Committee. Chairmen in any event have less power. Congressional party leaders have less influence. Congressional staffs are larger and more assertive. Committee hearings and discussions on sensitive foreign policy issues are less often closed to the public and press.

Frequently the result is deadlock, delay, more opportunities for obstruction, more fragmentation of responsibility, and less possibility that the United States can speak abroad with one consistent and authoritative voice. But the result is also more open, accountable, democratic decision-making—a foreign policy more responsive to public views. The American public, according to the polls, has heard the criticism of congressional "interference" in foreign affairs but does not endorse it.

Outside of government, the foreign policy "elite" or establishment once numbering at most in the hundreds—"the closest thing to a governing aristocracy that has survived in American democracy," in the words of Richard Reeves—now consists of thousands. Once largely confined to the Washington-New York-Boston corridor, it is now found in all parts of the country. Once led mostly by Protestant white male graduates of Ivy League universities with close family and business ties, it is now (like the U.S. Foreign Service, the Council on Foreign Relations and the Ivy League itself) more representative of all those citizens, regardless of race, gender and social position, who know and care about foreign affairs. Once focused primarily on our relations with Western Europe and Moscow, it now includes specialists on Latin America, the Middle East, East Asia, Africa, and other parts of the globe. Once the elite shared a bipartisan cold war consensus, based on the undisputed need to contain Stalinist expansion, on the memory of pre-World War II appeasement and lack of preparedness, and on the deep conviction that America had a special moral responsibility of worldwide dimensions. Now a new and expanded elite, which includes representatives of the "neo-conservative" Republican right and the "new politics" Democratic left (neither of whom shares the old elite's attachment to the Atlantic Alliance), agrees on very little.

One of the last public parades of the old elite was the collection of former secretaries and under secretaries of state and defense, former CIA directors and national security advisors and other former officials who gathered in 1971 to oppose the Mansfield Amendment reducing U.S. troop levels in Europe. "It looks to me like the resurrection of the Old Guard," commented Senator Mansfield. "It took me back 20 or 25 years . . . but this issue will not disappear."[8]

History and heritage drew Western Europe closely to the old foreign policy Establishment—men like Acheson, Lovett, Marshall, Dulles, Herter, McCloy and Stevenson. But today they are largely gone, replaced by a new and less influential foreign policy establishment that has few ties to the founding of the Atlantic Alliance and is competing for power and attention in a country whose presidential politics in recent decades has been in another of its antiestablishment phases. Johnson, Nixon, Ford, Carter and Reagan were not from the Northeast, the Ivy League, or the Council on Foreign Relations. Nor were they—with the exception of Nixon—experienced in international affairs. Instead, they often invoked traditional populist themes that appealed to the public distrust of diplomats, bureaucrats, academics and other establishmentarians.

It was neither surprising nor undemocratic that greater influ-

---

[8]*Congressional Quarterly Almanac, 1971*, Washington, D.C.: Congressional Quarterly, Inc., 1971, pp. 273, 275.

ence over U.S. foreign policy during the first two postwar decades was exercised by those who were particularly interested in
it over a sustained period because of their long study and experience. To the extent, however, that this informed elite saluted
"the people" only in theory, while mistrusting and excluding
their judgment in practice, its inflated share of influence on the
pyramid could not be maintained. Several separate but converg-
ing trends reduced its monopoly while broadening its base: the
sharp increase in this country's level of education, international
tourism and foreign business; the increasing sophistication and
use by politicians of published and private surveys of American
public opinion on all issues, including foreign policy; the in-
voluntary exposure of tens of millions of Americans to foreign
affairs developments through television, as discussed below;
the dramatic increase in the number of presidential nominating
primaries in which foreign policy issues were debated at the
grassroots; and the intense public feelings about these issues
aroused by the war in Vietnam. Especially after Watergate's
spotlight on the abuses of the "Imperial Presidency" and the
post-Watergate investigation of intelligence agency abuses, it
was no longer possible to defend an executive branch monopoly
on information and power that had previously prevented public
or even congressional knowledge of certain combat operations
and commitments. Even the future of the Atlantic Alliance, with
its effectiveness ultimately dependent upon U.S. public support, could have been jeopardized by the continuation of that
exclusionist approach.

Today the American public is heard on foreign policy—
through political action committees, opinion polls, petitions, let-
ters to editors and congressmen, editorial and "Op-Ed" essays,
pressure groups, protest demonstrations and otherwise, com-
municating directly with the president and secretary of state or
indirectly through Congress. Presidents have learned that their
decisions on war and peace no longer enjoy the automatic pass-
ive support of a citizen majority and are not long sustainable
without that majority support. Far more than ever before, public
acceptability has become an important U.S. foreign policy criter-
ion.

It is hypocritical to dismiss as elitism West European fears that a more democratic American foreign policy will become too political, emotional, forgetful, inflexible, inconsistent and unpredictable, less professional than a policy controlled by the few, less well informed, less likely to take the long view. The old establishment imposed a kind of moral authority on foreign policy decision-making that could override ideological, partisan and self-serving interests. Because meaningful public opinion is too often formed only after the crucial decisions have already been made and their results known, scholar and White House assistant Emmet Hughes once observed that "opinion polls provide only post mortem facts to those involved in pre-partum deliberations." Much earlier, Walter Lippmann, a supporter of the old elite, wrote harshly:

> The unhappy truth is that the prevailing public opinion has been destructively wrong at the critical junctures. The people have . . . compelled the governments, which usually knew what would have been wiser, or was necessary, or was more expedient, to be too late with too little, or too long with too much, too pacifist in peace and too bellicose in war, too neutralist or appeasing in negotiation or too intransigent. Mass opinion has acquired mounting power in this century. It has shown itself to be a dangerous master of decisions when the stakes are life and death.[9]

Objective surveys show that much of the American public is still ill informed, often handicapped by stereotypes and slogans even on those issues on which strong opinions are expressed, usually uninterested in seeking more information, and consistently unconcerned about most foreign policy issues, particularly in comparison with the domestic economy. A Chicago Council on Foreign Relations series of parallel polls of the general public and the informed elite indicated that the latter were more international-minded, more concerned about Soviet expansionism, more supportive of U.S. troops defending Western Europe against a Soviet invasion, more attentive to Alliance issues, less protectionist, less opposed to foreign aid, but not—contrary to the accusation heard in some quarters—invariably

---

[9]*Essays in the Public Philosophy,* Boston: Little, Brown, 1955, p. 20.

more hawkish. The general public was more willing than the elite to send troops to save Poland, for example, more concerned about communism in areas peripheral to U.S. interests, and less favorably inclined toward U.S.-Soviet arms control and other forms of cooperation.

The picture is not all bleak. Most members of the general public are not as ideological as are many large sectors of the leadership elite, and not as bogged down with excessive jargon and inapt analogies. American public opinion, as noted in more detail below, has been remarkably consistent in its adherence to most basic long-range foreign policy objectives and remarkably supportive of our unprecedented commitment to defend Western Europe. Neither unilateralist nor isolationist, preferring neither a weak nor a belligerent America, it has been selective in its endorsement of armed intervention and steadfast in its support of human rights and negotiated solutions. Most presidents who achieve results within those boundaries can still draw upon a large reservoir of public confidence without needing to justify their every tactic. If adequately informed about an issue over a prolonged period, the American people are likely to support a decision that is reasonable and realistic.

"If adequately informed. . . ." That is the problem; and solving that problem has been both facilitated and complicated by a revolutionary change since NATO's founding in the chief source of the American public's information about foreign affairs. In 1950, nine percent of American homes had a television set—today 98 percent do. Television became the primary provider of news for most Americans in 1963, and its lead has continued to increase ever since. Television news is the principal source of information for most people on presidential and congressional elections, foreign policy, international conflicts and other national and international events. Evening news shows in particular—including the news telecast on local stations, many of which have extensive foreign coverage and even their own foreign correspondents—are watched by more than seven of every ten American adults in the course of a week. Network television news alone reaches over 50 million viewers on an average week night.

Satellite broadcasting, electronic hand-held cameras, videotape and other technological advances have steadily increased live television news coverage of overseas events, particularly in Western Europe where more television bureaus are stationed than in any other foreign region. From time to time events in Vietnam, Iran, Israel and Lebanon have logically received more U.S. television news attention than Western Europe; and the Soviet Union not surprisingly is consistently a lead topic. But events in Western Europe have over the years occupied a sizable share of the foreign affairs coverage on network television news.

On a proportionate basis, compared to the 10 to 25 percent of general interest news that most newspapers typically devote to international events (even *The New York Times* coverage rarely exceeds 40 percent), the roughly 45 percent of news time devoted on the average by the networks to foreign affairs is impressive. But 45 percent of the 22 minutes of news contained in a 30 minute newscast does not convey enough words to fill one-third of one page of a standard-size newspaper, much less adequately inform the public about a large and complex world. One analysis of post-election surveys in 1948 (when print media dominated the news) and 1976 (when television news was dominant, and public affairs programming had doubled) concluded that public understanding of the issues had not noticeably improved.

But three important differences make television's impact on American attitudes toward foreign policy much greater than print journalism has ever had. First, a far higher proportion of Americans watch television news than ever read newspapers or news magazines. Second, live action pictures on television give it a credibility and impact, according to surveys, that overrides any conflicting information received from newspapers—or the president, the State Department, congressional leaders and private organizations. Rightly or wrongly, the viewing public strongly believes that television is ably and adequately "covering" the news.

Third, and most significant, television reaches a huge "inadvertent" audience, those at the bottom of the foreign policy power pyramid who are normally uninterested in world events. Newspaper surveys find very few consumers reading very few foreign news stories for more than a very few minutes. Most of those who do read foreign news read only headlines and an occasional half of a story, and make clear that they do not want more foreign news coverage. The average newspaper reader reads even less. But the average television viewer, who spends one-third of his day watching the screen "by the hour instead of by program," is exposed involuntarily to international news that he would not have chosen to learn. The members of this vast inadvertent audience, many of whom have little or no information on the world beyond our borders other than that conveyed to them by television, often find their attention unintentionally engaged by the picture unfolding before them, their interest aroused, their opinions formed, and their actions as voters and citizens motivated.

Extending participation in foreign policy decision-making to those at the bottom of the pyramid is undoubtedly democratic; but whether it results in wise and constructive decisions depends on the adequacy and accuracy of the information they receive. If the limitations of a 100-second news story require oversimplified presentations of multifaceted problems and the total omission of less dramatic events, if the limitations of the camera require the slighting of key institutional and evolutionary developments that are better analyzed in print, if for the sake of a good picture a negative emphasis on colorful violence and dramatic conflict exaggerates the role of force in the world, then those television viewers with few or no other sources of information may urge undeservedly hasty or deceptively painless decisions upon their government.

Television, moreover, lends itself even less than newspapers to the encouragement of secret or even quiet diplomacy, the kind in which compromises are painstakingly negotiated to completion before second-guessing criticism can undermine them. Television helps to publicize plans or intentions that might better have been left unknown, to spread words of anger or commitment that might better have been left unheard. "I doubt," said Abba Eban, the former Foreign Minister of Israel, "whether . . . Moses on Mount Sinai would have been . . . [successful] if, after every one of the Ten Commandments, he had to come down . . . and be interviewed by Walter Cronkite or Barbara Walters."[10]

But, for better or worse, television has greatly increased the democratization of American foreign policy. It has reduced the influence of *The New York Times* and *The Washington Post*, the daily journals of the old foreign policy establishment. It has communicated many a breaking international event to the entire nation at virtually the identical moment that the president and director of the CIA learn about it. Its in-depth public affairs programs have informed more people about more foreign problems than any other medium in history. It has brought to millions the expert foreign policy views of public officials and private scholars, including many who would never have been invited to join the old elite. It has required the U.S. government to present appealing reasons for any course of action abroad that will cause public alarm. And it has given all U.S. citizens, regardless of the regional influences to which they are subject or the newspaper markets in which they live, the same information on foreign affairs at the same time.

Contrary to the fears of many Europeans, increased democratization of U.S. foreign policy has not led to discontinuity. To be sure, one recent president decried America's "inordinate fear of Communism," while his successor condemned the Soviet Union as an "evil empire." One condemned all human rights violations, the other only those committed by "totalitarian" as distinguished from "authoritarian" states.

But the fundamental objectives of American foreign policy directly affecting the Atlantic Alliance have not basically changed through eight presidents and four decades. Tactics may change. Priorities may change. New weapons systems rise, fall, and rise again. A revised national security policy may change less than ten percent of the defense budget. New presidents may begin their terms with proposals for sweeping change that the practical responsibilities of leadership in the real world soon modify. But our national commitment to the Atlantic Alliance as an indis-

---

[10]"Interest and Conscience in Modern Diplomacy," Morgenthau Memorial Lecture on Morality and Foreign Policy, Council for Religion and International Affairs, New York, N.Y., December 4, 1984, p. 6.

pensable defender of common Western values and security, our commitment to resist Soviet incursions on the frontiers of freedom, our determination to assure the substantial equivalence (not superiority) of NATO military might and readiness in comparison with those of the Warsaw Pact, and our recognition of the futility, immorality and unwinnability of nuclear war, have not changed, presidential speeches and expert pronouncements to the contrary notwithstanding.

Despite a recent wave of volatility regarding particular issues and candidates, my long-term analysis of opinion polls and party platforms shows similar constancy at the grassroots. A preference for negotiation over confrontation, a disdain for regimes violating human rights, and a commitment to collective security have been the consistent findings of virtually every American public opinion poll since the Second World War. Planks praising the Atlantic Alliance, calling for its revitalization and blaming the other party for its deficiencies have been included, however, briefly and routinely, in virtually every national platform of both major political parties over the same period.

In the final analysis, the democratization of foreign policy decision-making in this country, for all its limitations, is not an issue for debate. It is a fact of life to which Alliance supporters, on both sides of the Atlantic, must adjust.

Vietnam

Millions of words have been written, many in the tenth anniversary year of the American withdrawal from the war in Vietnam, regarding the lessons of that tragic conflict. But little agreement exists. Not one of the many factions drawing their own separate lessons can prove the validity of its conclusions or disprove anyone else's. Even agreement on what happened and why still eludes us. An increasing percentage of the American public, according to the polls, now concludes that we should never have intervened. But, as noted above, poll results should be read with care. The very question often suggests the answer; and my study of a dozen polls on Vietnam convinces me that most respondents are willing to affirm as the "lesson of Vietnam" almost any reasonable-sounding declaration on the interviewer's prepared list.

Disagreement over the lessons and meaning of Vietnam, however, does not eradicate its impact. It was a traumatic experience in the life of this country to lose a major war, to lose over 50,000 lives and countless limbs in the process, to subject 500,000 young American servicemen to extreme hazard and suffering, to alienate thousands of other young Americans (and their parents) who protested the war, and to bring all this bloodshed and bitterness into millions of American homes on television each night in living color.

The Vietnam War played a major role in nearly all of the changes discussed above. Congressional and public resentment of presidential leadership during the war increased the assertiveness of the legislative branch in foreign affairs, increased the democratization of foreign policy decision-making, and increased the antipathy to and limitations on secrecy. Television news and public opinion polls took on new importance. Resentment over the non-support of key allies, less attention to concerns across the Atlantic, a yearning by some for a return to isolationism, the argument that U.S. troops in Europe were needed elsewhere—all of these developments were stirred by American reaction to the war.

Of particular significance and concern to many in Europe was the extent to which the old postwar bipartisan consensus, organized essentially around the cold war call to contain Soviet expansion, was in the late 1960s splintered into a host of ideological, regional and other factions by bitterly divided reactions to our escalating involvement in Vietnam. Despite the continuing proclivity of American politicians and scholars to assume the voice of a unified nation ("the United States believes . . . the American people demand"),[11] that lack of true consensus on foreign policy continues today. Disagreements abound between

---

[11] The same error occurs in writings—including this one—that attribute particular views to "Western Europe," which suffers from even greater factionism and lack of consensus than the United States.

the president and Congress, between the House and Senate, within the executive branch, within each house of Congress, and within each of the two major political parties, reflecting similar disagreements among the voters at large. Most majority votes or views today, in either the Congress or the public, are comprised of disparate minorities. The "internationalist" majority previously discussed, for example, includes sharply different views on interventionism, unilateralism, protectionism, U.S.-Soviet relations, Central America and the Middle East.

Indeed, given these divisions and the need to debate them in a democracy, it seems remarkable that the previous consensus (even though it was shaped by fewer people, as was discussed) lasted for 20 years. It also seems unlikely that such a consensus will ever return with its former vigor in the absence of some extraordinarily unifying external threat.

Because the establishment of the Atlantic Alliance was one of the crowning achievements of that earlier American consensus, the Vietnam-induced demise of that consensus has understandably caused grave concern among Europeans who question the United States' continuing effectiveness as a steady world leader and reliable ally. Indeed, a lack of continuity, consistency and predictability in American foreign policy seems almost inevitable to many Europeans, who have long taken a dim view of our seemingly endless presidential campaigns and transitions and our peculiar electoral and governmental systems. But those peculiar systems, in the post-Vietnam absence of consensus, have served to resist drastic upheaval and have maintained, beneath the veneer of changing presidential emphasis and political debate, the remarkable continuity in the basic direction of American foreign policy previously cited.

It has also become commonplace, in Europe as well as the United States, to equate America's "Vietnam syndrome" with a policy of absolute nonintervention, if not outright isolationism. That greatly oversimplifies the posture of those to whom it is ascribed. Certainly the Vietnam experience reminded both "hawks" and "doves" of the limits of American military power and the horrors of modern war. Presidents and politicians no longer promise to "pay any price, bear any burden, meet any hardship, support any friend, [or] oppose any foe." Americans now are more inclined to distinguish between areas of vital importance to our security and those not worth the amount of blood, money and moral structure expended in Vietnam.

But to adopt discretion, caution and selectivity in the use of force is not to renounce it forever. Few Americans believe that this country should now shrink from its global responsibilities and interests, at the risk of seeing the rest of the world dominated by a hostile power, or believe that the use or threat of force has no role in meeting those responsibilities. As Republican Senator William Cohen of Maine has said: "The legacy of Vietnam does not mean that we will not send our sons anywhere. It does mean that we will not send them everywhere."[12] The post-Vietname debate asks where and when American military intervention is prudent, appropriate and effective; how to define our vital interests; and how to measure genuine threats. These are the questions; there is no consensus on the answers.

The two recent documents most heatedly criticized for attempting to spell out the answers were the 1984 National Democratic Party Platform and an address by Republican Secretary of Defense Weinberger on November 18, 1984. The two documents contain some remarkable similarities, perhaps indicating thereby the criteria most likely to be applied by any president in this century. Both would limit intervention to situations where America's vital national interests are directly threatened, where the use of combat force is a last resort, and where the objectives of our intervention are clear and attainable. The Democratic platform, attacked by conservatives as "neoisolationist," added a preference for multilateral action with our allies. The Weinberger "doctrine," to the public dismay of Secretary of State George Shultz but with the support of Vietnam-hardened officers in the Pentagon, added the importance of assured public and congressional support.

This last test was reinforced by former National Security Advisor Robert C. McFarlane's observation that the most relevant lesson he learned from Vietnam was "what is and what isn't sustainable by the American people. . . . Five years is simply incompatible with American values and the American attention

---

[12]George J. Church, "Lessons from a Lost War," *Time,* April 15, 1985, p. 40.

span."[13] A U.S. president weighing a potentially long-term intervention abroad, in short, must consider not only its merits in light of the lessons he has drawn from Vietnam but also its long-term acceptability to the American people in light of the lessons *they* have drawn; and what lessons they have drawn are still unclear.

It is erroneous, however, to exaggerate the impact of Vietnam. The American public still supports the dispatch of troops overseas in vital situations, and includes the defense of Europe at the top of its list. The loss in Vietnam did not diminish this country's relative economic strength and leadership in the world or its ties with other democracies. Even without the Vietnam experience, the growth of Soviet power and Third World independence would still have limited any U.S. role as world policeman; U.S. powerlessness in the face of such setbacks as the invasion of Afghanistan, the bombing of American embassies and the seizure of American hostages would still have impaired U.S. self-confidence; and the power of the old, more narrow foreign policy establishment would still have faded in our more egalitarian society. Even before the Vietnam experience, Congress had been unwilling to send troops to fight Nazi Germany until the United States was attacked; a substantial proportion of the U.S. population turned against U.S. military intervention in Korea; that latter war had taught many military leaders to avoid becoming bogged down in a long conflict on the Asian mainland without united support at home; and intense disputes over Cuba, China, and other issues over the years had indicated severe limitations on the exalted bipartisan consensus.

Moreover, as earlier noted, Americans today continue to support the same basic objectives they supported before Vietnam, including the Atlantic Alliance. Although the popular Grenada invasion was too quick and easy to test long-term public attitudes, recent polls indicate that the effects as well as the memory of the Vietnam War are fading, that restraints on the use of power are weakening, and that a substantial proportion of the U.S. population cannot even remember which side we supported in Vietnam. Also, as earlier noted, isolationist and uni-

---

[13] *The Wall Street Journal*, February 11, 1985.

lateralist attitudes peaked in the mid-1970s and have since declined.

Almost surely, division and doubt created by the Vietnam trauma will continue to hinder a full American foreign policy consensus for many more years. Our European allies must recognize this change. But the paralyzing guilt that the Vietnam War initially produced in some quarters of the U.S. population, the poisonous recriminations, and the angry urge to withdraw with revulsion from any multilateral obligation, have all substantially subsided.

The New Generation

In 1985 the President of the United States, Vice President, White House Chief of Staff, Secretary of State, Secretary of Defense, Speaker of the House and many key leaders of the executive and legislative branches had all served in the U.S. armed forces during the Second World War that had ended 40 years earlier. That war, the unsuccessful appeasement of Hitler at Munich that preceded it, and the ruthless acquisition of Eastern Europe by Stalin that followed it, were the defining events that shaped their views of the world and their support of the postwar Atlantic Alliance.

But in the United States today, as in Western Europe and Moscow, a new generation of leaders is beginning to emerge. Nearly 60 percent of the current members of the U.S. Senate and over 70 percent of the House of Representatives were not even of voting age when the NATO treaty was signed in 1949. Between the 1970 and 1980 elections the number of first-term congressmen and senators sharply increased, and the average age of those newly elected sharply decreased. Reflecting the growing power of younger members in both houses, nearly one-half of the seats on the House Foreign Affairs Committee, nearly one-third on the House Armed Services Committee, and nearly one-fourth on the Senate Foreign Relations and Armed Services Committees are occupied by men and women who were not even born the year before Pearl Harbor.

Different demographers use different cut-off ages; but it is clear that there are at least 60 million to 70 million potential American voters in the group dubbed by some as the "successor generation" (those roughly aged from 30 to 40 today); also known as the "Vietnam generation," because most of them reached draft age between the dates of the first and last American casualties in Vietnam; and also known as the "baby boomer" generation, because most of them reflect the decade-long surge in birth statistics that began after the close of World War II. (Also enjoying a brief fad was the term "yuppie," an acronymn for young urban professionals, which in truth defines only a small portion of this group.) Because this new generation was preceded and followed by much smaller generations, its sheer size could potentially dominate American politics, media, academia and opinion for many years to come.

Who are they? What has shaped their thinking? Only five percent of them are Vietnam war veterans; but that war, not World War II, was their entire generation's defining foreign policy experience. They comprise the best educated and most widely travelled generation in history, more familiar than their parents with European sports like soccer and cycling, with European culture on television and in the theater, and even with European-style cooking and architecture. More accustomed than their elders to the use of imported products, more likely to be working in a service industry where both unionism and protectionism are less dominant, they apply open and inquiring minds to those public policy issues that interest them.

But their sheer numbers flooding the labor market in the economically stagnant 1970s required them to make job security, not foreign policy or public affairs, their first priority. In 1980, for example, the number of American graduate students seeking a master's degree in geography, history or international relations had declined in comparison with 1965, despite an enormous rise in student enrollment, while the number seeking a master's degree in business and management had increased nearly eightfold.

The members of this generation have never known life without television, without the potential threat of nuclear destruction, and without the United States continuing to arm against the Soviet Union while treating the defense of Western Europe as the defense of our own country (once an unprecedented concept). They cannot remember World War II, the isolationism and appeasement that preceded it, or the postwar world in which Western Europe was weak, impoverished, and looking to the United States for leadership and help. Nor do they remember when or why NATO was founded, or a time when Europe and Germany were not divided by an Iron Curtain. The "cold war era," they were taught, was an unfortunate chapter in history.

In this context, what fundamental alterations can be expected in America's basic attitude toward the world, the Soviets and the Atlantic Alliance, once this new successor generation is in full command? *None.* This answer will disappoint and be disputed by some pop sociologists who have foretold wondrous changes when power passes to this group. But it is a "group" only in terms of demographics, not foreign policy. There are more fundamental differences in views among the members of this successor generation than between that generation and its elders.

The "gender gap" on presidential candidates and war and peace issues, and similar racial, religious, regional and other divisions, on candidates and issues, were all more marked in the 1984 election than any "generation gap." Occupation, income and education are more likely to matter than age in predicting an individual's response to foreign policy questions in opinion polls; and this is even more true of the informed and attentive elite than of the general population. The coming new wielders of power are as unlikely to reknit a foreign policy consensus among themselves as were their predecessors; and all generalizations about their views (including those set forth above and below) should be skeptically received.

True, the Vietnam War was a formative event for this generation. But it formed divisions, not unity. Youthful demonstrators made headline news; but a majority of their peers were either endorsing the war, accepting it, or regretting both the war and the demonstrations. A 1970 Gallup Poll, for example, found support among college students for immediate withdrawal of all troops from Vietnam to be slightly less than the one-fifth of all adults favoring that action. No doubt some of the new U.S. congressmen and governors who saw service in Vietnam are more likely to favor U.S. military intervention elsewhere on the basis of that experience; but others, as retired General Andrew Good-paster put it, are "less inclined to talk blithely of 'brush-fire' and 'limited wars' after seeing their men killed in battle."[14]

It is not a generation hell-bent to change the world, the views or the institutions that they inherited from their parents. The majority of the American public today, as noted by the polls previously cited, is strongly internationalist, mildly non-interventionist, deeply concerned about nuclear weapons and war, and clearly more interested in negotiations than confrontation—and that is true of the successor generation, only more so. Majority opinion today is more confident than it was five to ten years ago, most aware of our economic vulnerability in a competitive world, and less traumatized by the memory of Vietnam—all true as well of the successor generation, only more so. Public opinion today would support the defense of Europe against Soviet attack and, while wishing our allies would do more, remains willing to maintain American forces in Europe for as long as they are needed—and this, too, is true of the members of the successor generation, only more so.

The very term successor generation, implying a cohesive political group with consistent views, is misleading; for its members do not constitute a political monolith. Turned off by the traditional Democratic Party emphasis on a regulated economy as well as the new Republican Party attempts to intrude into their personal decision-making on such issues as family planning, school prayer, and censorship, they are not yet permanently and overwhelmingly wedded to any political party. Many are registered Democrats who voted for Reagan, despite disliking his views on war and civil rights. Most are independent ticket-splitters wary of virtually any political authority, organization or institution. Many have no wish to be political successors. The idealism exhibited by millions of them in the civil rights and peace drives of the 1960s was turned in many cases to cynicism and disillusionment by the war, Watergate, the Kennedy and King assassinations, and a series of disappointing presidencies.

---

[14]Michael Wright, "National Security's New Insiders," *The New York Times Magazine,* March 3, 1985, p. 62.

Neither the extreme left, the extreme right, nor any other ideological dogma appears to attract the majority of this notably pragmatic generation. They see no inconsistency in supporting both free enterprise and pollution control, both a strong defense and arms control, both a more compassionate government and less welfare spending. Unmoved by speeches about communist devils, they seem more willing than their elders to live-and-let-live with the Soviet Union and Cuba as we now do with China and Yugoslavia. Too young to remember the postwar era in which U.S. views generally prevailed, they appear less disillusioned by the persistence of adversity in today's unruly world. Those West Europeans who have long disdained the moralistic (as distinct from idealistic) messages and ideological tone of most American foreign policy rhetoric are likely to find the Vietnam generation's approach both refreshing and reassuring.

All this is not to say that the next leadership wave will not want to rearrange the furniture somehow, in government and foreign policy, as each successive wave has in the past. Senator Gary Hart, for example, who became for a brief period in the 1984 primaries the presidential standard-bearer for the successor generation, called for military reform in NATO as well as the Pentagon, for a new focus on international economic competition, and for an allied contingency plan for the Persian Gulf. But his "new ideas" theme did not extend to support for the Nunn Amendment or to any weakening of our NATO commitment. The successor generation is not determined to alter Atlantic relations.

Nevertheless, during this generation's formative years, the threat of war and Soviet opportunism arose repeatedly in the Third World but never in Europe, where NATO's strength and Moscow's unreliable East European allies have made any Soviet invasion or even miscalculation appear increasingly unlikely. The Atlantic Alliance has thus sometimes seemed to many of this group a distant anachronism, once of interest to the old establishment but now a source of squabbles and financial drain.

It is simply not their concern in foreign policy, as reflected in the speeches of their leaders. A survey of *The Congressional Record*, campaign speeches and other addresses found far more references to Europe and NATO in the remarks of Walter Mondale than in those of Gary Hart, Bill Bradley, Jack Kemp and Richard Gephardt combined. It is, in short, a generation that may well be the first to ask why—the strategic conditions and assumptions underlying NATO having drastically changed since 1949—the basic security commitments first made at that time should not also be reexamined.

III. The Reexamination Ahead

This is not cause for alarm. Reexamination does not automatically mean rejection. I am confident, as the foregoing indicates, that a fresh look by a new group of American leaders at the premises on which the Alliance was founded need not be poisoned by either right-wing unilateralism or left-wing isolationism, by a prejudice in favor of the Pacific Basin or against Europe's economic status, or by threats to withdraw our troops across the Atlantic. But to survive that reexamination, as also indicated above, the case for the Alliance must make sense to the democratic many and not merely to the dedicated establishment few. It must meet the post-Vietnam test of selectivity and the new generation's test of pragmatism. It must offer something more than a rehash of old and familiar goals.

The formulation of new Alliance goals and principles are beyond the scope of this book. Permit me to suggest simply and broadly that the Alliance will need in this new era a new and less dangerous strategy for East-West relations, new forms of cooperation not limited to the military and diplomatic sphere, a broader partnership that extends beyond our common fears to serve our common political, economic and cultural interests.

That is surely not beyond the imagination or reach of the talented and energetic young men and women now rising to responsibility in Western capitals—particularly if those talents can be devoted to creating new instruments of statecraft instead of warfare and if that energy can be focused on boosting internationalism instead of nationalism.

But it will require high level collaboration, not U.S. dictation— more than the collaboration now exhibited in the routine speeches and pre-cooked communiqués of the "photo opportunity" extravaganza known as the annual Western economic summit. It will require recognition that not every legitimate allied difference of perspective is tantamount to disarray and not every disarray is an Atlantic crisis. Neither differences nor even disarray are new or cause for panic. In terms of harmony, NATO will never match the Warsaw Pact. Shared values do not mean identical economic and political interests and responsibilities. Differences between the United States and the European Community, between NATO goals and commitments, and between commitments and capabilities, have often arisen in the past and will arise again in the future. Disagreements over weapons productions and standardization, demonstrations against missile deployment, disappointments over leaks or speeches—none of this is unprecedented or surprising.

As earlier noted, history and geography gave Europe and America different views on issues ranging from East-West trade to arms control to Third World revolutions. Neither the United States nor Western Europe should expect automatic support from the other on all issues, in or out of Alliance jurisdiction. Atlantic unity is not an end in itself but a means, an essential instrument, to help obtain a secure and peaceful Europe.

Neither paralyzed by, nor indifferent to, these differences between us, both the United States and Europe can manage them better. A more sensitive, empathetic America could try fewer self-satisfied lectures and more advance consultation, fewer threats about burden-sharing and more effort toward arms control. A less pessimistic, more unified Western Europe could remove the protectionist mote from its own eye while noting America's, increase its own contribution to the cost of equipping and housing the NATO troops required for its defense, and emphasize to its own demonstrators that only increased conventional readiness will raise the nuclear threshold that they never want to cross. The pace of political and economic integration, and the "Europeanization" of Europe, can only come from Europe; but we in this country can make more clear than we have that we welcome that process and its benefits for Alliance decision-making.

All this can and must be done over the next decade by new leaders on both sides of the Atlantic. On our side, leadership in placing these matters before the Congress and public in the proper perspective can come only from the president. That is one difference that can truly make a difference.

Recent Publications of the
Council on Foreign Relations

Trade Talks: America Better Listen!, C. Michael Aho and Jonathan David Aronson, Council on Foreign Relations, 1985.

Compact for African Development, Committee on African Development Strategies, Council on Foreign Relations in conjunction with the Overseas Development Council, 1985.

Latin Migration North: The Problem for U.S. Foreign Policy, Michael S. Teitelbaum, Council on Foreign Relations, 1985.

Third World Instability: Central America As A European-American Issue, Andrew J. Pierre, editor, Council on Foreign Relations, 1985.

India and the United States, Council on Foreign Relations, 1985.

Ripe for Resolution: Conflict and Intervention in Africa, I. William Zartman, Oxford University Press, 1985.

Arms and the African: The Military Influences on Africa's International Relations, William J. Foltz and Henry S. Bienen, eds., Yale University Press, 1985.

Canada and the United States: Enduring Friendship, Persistent Stress, John H. Sigler and Charles F. Doran, eds., Prentice-Hall, 1985. •

A Changing Israel, Peter Grose, Vintage Books/Random House, 1985.

Prospects for Peace in the Middle East: The View From Israel, A Conference Report, Council on Foreign Relations, 1985.

For complete catalog and ordering information please contact Publications Office, Council on Foreign Relations, 58 East 68th Street, New York, N.Y., 10021. (212) 734–0400.